**IRINODA, Colour Atlas and Criteria
of Fundus Changes in Hypertension**

ERRATA IN CAPTIONS

Page	Wrong	Correct
60	pararell-Gunn's	parallel-Gunn's
68	Punctiforme	Punctiform

COLOUR ATLAS AND CRITERIA OF FUNDUS CHANGES IN HYPERTENSION

Research Staffs on "Hypertensive Fundus"
by Grantees Ministry of Education

Chief **KIMIHO IRINODA**, M. D.

(Professor of Hirosaki University)

IGAKU SHOIN LTD. TOKYO

J. B. LIPPINCOTT COMPANY
PHILADELPHIA AND TORONTO

Sole Distributor in the United States and Canada
J. B. LIPPINCOTT COMPANY, East Washington Square, Philadelphia Pa., U. S. A.

Printed and Bound in Japan

Foreword

In hypertensive disease, the ocular fundus examination is at the present time a common procedure and it is also common to use photographs so as to obtain objectivity as well as to contribute to the diagnosis of the process.

However, when we write down the fundus findings in a word or dispose of them statistically, there is ambiguity and confusion which results in some differences of individual judgment, and expression of judgment itself. Therefore the value of the ocular fundus examination, which offers an important clue to the condition of the blood vessels of the whole body, has a tendency to be doubted and set at naught.

Professor IRINODA, pondering this fact, intended to publish various typical photographs of findings in hypertensive disease.

When we can resolve the ambiguity and confusion in recording the ocular fundus findings, I am sure we can get a better result than that of the classifications of KEITH-WAGENER and SCHEIE. This is very significant, so I heartily appreciate Professor IRINODA's excellent achievement.

These figures were chosen from some thousands of photographs of the ocular fundus, which were considered by the Hypertension Committee, which consists of a number of persons who have an interest in this realm. These figures are superior to those published in Europe and America; they might be called definitive figures.

We believe that people should have a deeper understanding of the essentials of hypertension, which is the most common disease. Persons who have a keen interest in this disease will especially appreciate the value of the ocular fundus examination.

SHIN-ICHI SHIKANO

—Tokyo University—

Members of Subcommittee

K. IRINODA, M.D.

S. MATSUYAMA, M.D.

F. HIJIKATA, M.D.

J. KUWAJIMA, M.D.

S. KIMURA, M.D.

K. KATOH, M.D.

M. MATSUI, M.D.

A. NAKAJIMA, M.D.

H. ARAI, M.D.

N. KUNITOMO, M.D.

M. UYAMA, M.D.

T. MIZUKAWA, M.D.

K. HARA, M.D.

H. IKUI, M.D.

Preface

It is well-known to all that ophthalmological observation plays a significant role as a kind of biopsy in the diagnosis and treatment of hypertension. In this article, hypertension refers to a disease in which there is an abnormal elevation of the brachial blood-pressure as a cardinal symptom, and includes hypertensive diseases that are due to various causes. From the very nature of things, the fundus view in hypertension has changes in the retinal arterioles as its main object, and presents ophthalmoscopically any similar change regardless of origin, the common mechanism being hypertonus. However, according to the basic diseases these changes vary greatly in length of progress, speed of course, grade of severity, and appearance of accompanying retinal lesions such as haemorrhage or white spots. Therefore accurate observation of the ophthalmoscopic findings is necessary for a practitioner. On the other hand, the study of fundus photographs had made progress since the development of the fundus camera by NORDENSON (1928) and has recently accelerated with the advancement of film techniques, gradually making possible recording in natural colour. At present, brief and complete recording of the fundus is widely practiced.

But, because the knowledge required to observe the findings and determine their meaning is incomplete, the clinical application has fallen short of our expectations.

Luckily the group discussion on the hypertensive fundus was set up in the XV Clinical Ophthalmological Meeting in 1961, and every year since then this meeting has been held for the purpose of the acquisition of mutual knowledge. Then, through the work of the excellent research staff on the synthetic study of "Hypertensive Fundus" as Grantees of the Ministry of Education clinical, histopathological, experimental, and hygienical researches progressed from 1963 to 1964. (Members : IRINODA, K., Hirosaki University ; NAKAJIMA, A., Juntendo University ; MIKUNI, M., Niigata University; KUNITOMO, N., Nihon University; KATOH, K., Nihon University; IKUI, H., Kyushu University; ASAYAMA, R., Kyoto University; KUWAJIMA, J., Tohoku University; MIZUKAWA, T., Osaka University; HIWATARI, S., Nihon Medical College; SATOH, K., Hirosaki University).

Thereafter the research group has continued its best efforts, holding annual or semiannual meetings, and in November 1966, after consultation, organized a committee for the purpose of determining diagnostic criteria (Staff : IRINODA, K.; KUWAJIMA, J.; KATOH, K.; KUNITOMO, N.; NAKAJIMA, A.; MIZUKAWA, T.; IKUI, H.; MATSUYAMA, S.; HIJIKATA, F.; KIMURA, S.; MATSUI, M.; ARAI, H.; UYAMA, M. and HARA, K.).

Through close cooperation in several meetings, we have formed a definite plan to determine the criteria and select standard slides. We have now published this colour atlas with diagnostic criteria.

The author hopes that a large number of subscribers will understand the work and make good use of this book.

May 25 th, 1970

KIMIHO IRINODA, M. D.

CONTENTS

Explanation

This book consists of a definition of ophthalmoscopical findings in hypertension, remarks on grading, and colour films illustrating fundus pathology. About 90 fundus photographs have been chosen in order that any person may recognize the cardinal changes, with photographs showing the principal points of these changes, so that the author need not add any additional commentary.

A few important points, resulting from several discussions, have been noted in this book; so the object of this book and its method of compilation have been clarified with the author's hope that this will substitute for explanatory remarks. The author is very grateful if this book is of any help to its readers.

1) Object of Publication

From April 1964 to April 1965, technical terms concerning hypertension were investigated by the "Ophthalmological Study on Hypertension" Research Group, for the purpose of correcting confusion and irregularity found in those terms used to designate fundus changes relative to elevation of the blood pressure. In the course of investigating these terms, to say nothing of the confusion in them, we found that the same terms have meanings which vary with the respective users. On the other hand, many differences in the diagnostic standards in grading have been clarified.

We learned that there were personnel in other fields of study (medicine and public health, for example) who wished to be able to know, more easily and precisely the criteria and fundus findings in hypertension, and their classification. Thus, we first decided to standardize the nomenclature of the respective fundus findings in hypertension in order to set up a definitively written standardization, which has resulted in the publication of this book. Therefore this book makes it possible for readers to grasp the fundus findings easily and know precisely how to describe the respective findings and to clarify their content by consulting this book.

2) Fundamental Principle of Compilation

This publication is not perfect; there are some points where we have tried to give the most adequate description of the subjects, from a scientific viewpoint, in their actual state. We want to clarify the essential points of compilation so that the reader may understand the above-mentioned view of ours.

(1) Setting up definitions to judge the fundus findings in essential and other types of hypertension.

(2) Setting up standardizations based on the ophthalmoscopic forms exclusively without taking into consideration histopathological or pathophysiological points in each finding. (Assigning meaning to the findings, at the present time, does not generally prevail, and we believe that there are many points to be researched in this field.)

(3) Concerning synthetic judgment, or grading of the fundus findings, we have only introduced or added the former classifications of fundus findings.

3) Narrowness-Existence or Non-Criterion of the Retinal Arterioles

The narrowness of retinal arterioles is classified, according to its appearance and extent; as diffuse, generalized narrowness and localized (circumscribed), or partial narrowness. Of these, localized narrowness being recognized as calibre-irregularity, it is not difficult to judge its extent. Concerning judgment of diffuse narrowness, several methods have been heretofore tried, but no satisfactory method applicable to all cases, is known. We finally adopted the judging method of Arterio-Venous Ratio (A/V) which has been used since the old days.

Concerning Arterio-Venous Ratio, we ordinarily choose an artery-vein pair to be compared; however, we have many cases that are impossible to judge, but this method has been adopted for the reason that it has the merit of needing no special instruments.

Considering that subdivision might result in incorrect judgment of grading, we classified the following: non narrowness (−), narrowness of slight grade (+), narrowness of moderate grade (++) and narrowness of severe grade (+++).

In case of judgments of narrowness, there is "an apparent narrowness" which needs particular attention. The retinal artery itself is not narrow; nevertheless when retinal oedema, and retinal exudate (which are changes in extra-vascular i. e. perivascular tissue) make the blood vessels appear narrowed, such a phenomenon is called "apparent narrowness". This has often caused some discussion in cases of calibre-irregularity. The "apparent narrowness" can be, to some extent, distinguished from the real narrowness by means of fluorescence fundus photography. If it is a real narrowness, it appears in this type of photo clearly.

Concerning functional narrowness and organic narrowness, these have been discussed in many books heretofore, yet in practical cases, the judgment of difference in the two types is hard to make. On the other hand, there are also some negative opinions regarding the view that the functional narrowness is in the retinal arteriole, and whether the spasm is in it or not.

After several discussions, we adopted our fundamental principle not to assign meanings to findings, as mentioned above. However, taking consideration of the blood vessels themselves and the circumstances, if there is difference between the two types, we are to record it.

We classified functional narrowness into functional narrowness in its narrowest sense and angiospastic narrowing; the judgment of which is very simply dependent upon haemorrhage, white spots and oedema which are the signs of organic changes. On the other hand, functional narrowness is considered similar to reversible narrowness. It should be repeatedly evaluated over a period of time. In such a case, it is better to observe the changes for some time by means of artery papillar ratio and vein papillar ratio than to observe them by means of the arteriovenous ratio. You can understand the functional status of the blood vessel by observing the retinal artery changes, as in the test of elevation of blood pressure by cold. It is desirable to use these as a supplementary diagnosis.

4) Reflex of Retinal Arterioles

It is difficult to set up general standards of judgment of the reflex-increase. In this book, we measured it by the width of the reflex-streak, the artery blood column ratio (AR/AC) and classified them in 3 grades: normal (−), slight increase (+), and great increase (+). AR/AC ratio 40~45 %, 45~50, 60 % and over, shown in the table, are quite approximate values. Such values were obtained from measurements of the fundus photographs in cases which we recognized as showing increase in the light reflex ophthalmoscopically.

Concerning copper-wired arteries and the silver-wired arteries, we have discussed whether we might adopt these terms or not, but finally we leave these words as technical terms, to show them in photographs.

5) Changes of the Vascular Course

Concerning straightening and tortuosity, setting aside their respective meanings, the value of arterio-venous tortuosity varies considerably physiologically in healthy individuals, according to the research of a few scholars(KINUKAWA and HAYAKAWA, etc).However, we have decided that only the extent of straightening and tortuosity is recognizable ophthalmo-scopically.

6) Arterio-Venous Crossing Phenomenon

The arterio-venous crossing phenomena can be rather minutely graded as follows: normal (−), slight (+), moderate (╫), severe (╫╫).

7) Abnormality of the Branching Angle

A good many differences, due to the vascular course, are found in branching angles of healthy persons. In extraordinary cases of branching angles, there are acute-angling and obtuse-angling, but we could not distinguish them in terms of numerical values. So we showed only the average value of the superior temporal artery (ARAI).

8) About other findings, we believe we have mentioned them in the section on definitions, so no more needs to be said here.

Changes in Arteriolar Calibre

Narrowness and narrowing of the arterioles
(Fig. 2)

In this paper, "narrowness" means the condition where the arterioles appear narrow or attenuated ophthalmologically, in comparison with their average size in normal individuals, irrespective of the cause and progressive course. On the other hand, "narrowing" means the condition where the arterioles get narrow or constrict pathologically, in comparison with their original (natural?) breadth in each individual.

1) Types of Arteriolar Narrowness
   A. Classification by ophthalmological appearance.
      (1) Narrowness with no irregularity in breadth (Fig. 3~5)
            ······generalized or diffuse narrowness of arterioles.

      (2) Narrowness with irregularity in breadth (Fig. 6~8)
            ······calibre-irregularity; classified by the type of irregularity in the outline of arterioles, as follows:

         a) localized or focal narrowness.   →

         b) segmental or segmentary narrowness.

                                                 →

         c) indentation.   →

         d) irregular narrowness.   →

   B. Classification by physico-pathological findings.
Ophthalmological views of arteriolar narrowness which may occur in physico-pathological conditions can be described as follows and may be classified conceptually and practically with reference to other ophthalmoscopic signs. However, there are some difficulties in differentiating one from another, clinically.

(1) Organic narrowness (Fig. 9, 10)=arteriolosclerotic narrowness.
Arteriolar narrowness accompanied by other signs of
arteriolar sclerosis.
(2) Functional narrowing (Fig. 11~14)=hypertonic narrowing (in a wide sense)
a) Hypertonic narrowing (in a narrow sense)
Arteriolar narrowing wherein no change occurs in
the retina besides that of the arterioles.
b) Angiospastic narrowing
Arteriolar narrowing of hypertonic type so severe
that it elicits functional or organic change in the
retinal tissue.
(3) Narrowness of mixed type (Fig. 15) = mixed type of 1)
and 2).

2) Grading and Its Assessment of Narrowness or Narrowing
  1. Narrowness or narrowing accompanied by no calibre-irregularity.
  i) The breadth of the arteriole is estimated with reference to
  normal relationship with the accompanying venule (A/V ratio).

Grade	Description	A/V ratio
Normal	(−)	3/4 ~ 2/3
Slight grade	(+)	2/3 ~ 1/2
Moderate grade	(⧺)	1/2 ~ 1/3
Severe grade	(⧻)	< 1/3

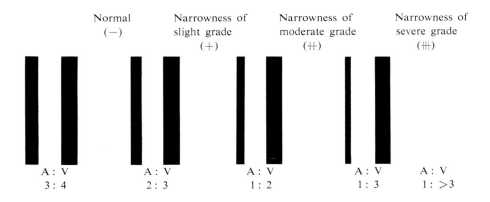

Normal (−)	Narrowness of slight grade (+)	Narrowness of moderate grade (⧺)	Narrowness of severe grade (⧻)
A : V 3 : 4	A : V 2 : 3	A : V 1 : 2	A : V 1 : 3 A : V 1 : >3

ii) When the size of one or both of the arteriolar branches peripheral to the ramification is half or less than that of the parent branch of the ramification, narrowness or narrowing is present.

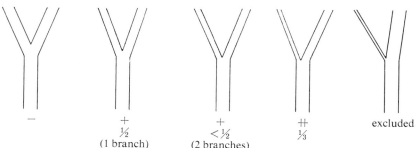

| − | +
½
(1 branch) | +
<½
(2 branches) | ++
⅓ | excluded |

2. Narrowness or narrowing accompanied by calibre-irregularity.

In comparing the breadth of the arteriole at the affected part with that at the adjacent and proximal part, grading and its assessment of narrowing is made as follows.

Assessment	Description	Ratio		
absent (normal)	8 −	No irregularity of outline		
slight	+	3/4∼1/2		
remarkable	++	less than 1/2		

In accordance with the above-mentioned criteria, the type, grade and site of narrowness or narrowing as well as the number of arterioles affected must be described; for example, three arterioles out of four (abbreviated as 4 (3)).

Note (Fig. 16,17):
1. Keep in mind that there are physiological variations in the size of the arteriole.
2. Differentiation is needed between narrowness in hypertensive diseases and that in cases of high myopy, pigmentary degeneration of the retina, and other vascular affections of the choroid.
3. The nasal branches of the retinal arterioles are anatomically narrower than the temporal ones.
4. Ophthalmoscopically-diagnosed narrowness may include apparent narrowness (cf. supplementary diagnostic methods).

Normal fundus

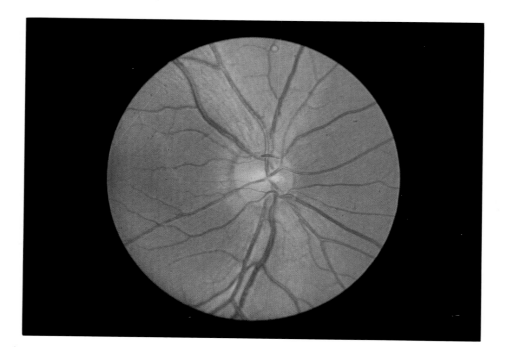

Fig. 1

Without arteriolar narrowness

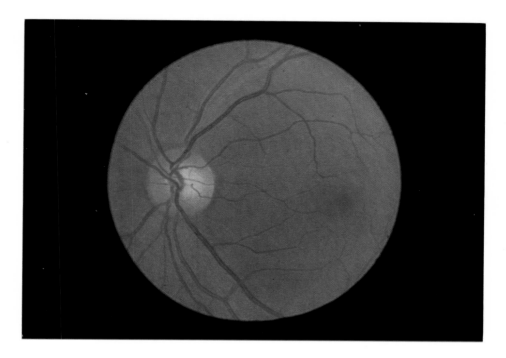

Fig. 2

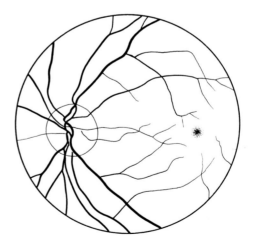

Generalized arteriolar narrowness (of slight grade)

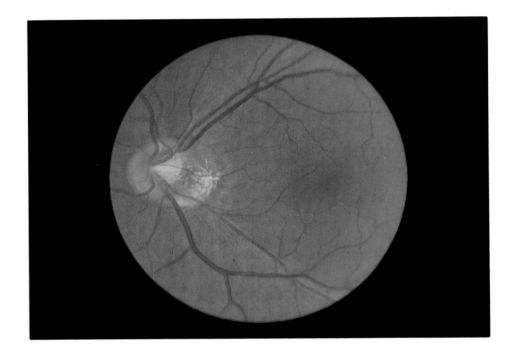

Fig. 3

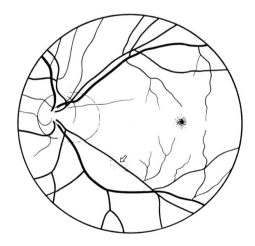

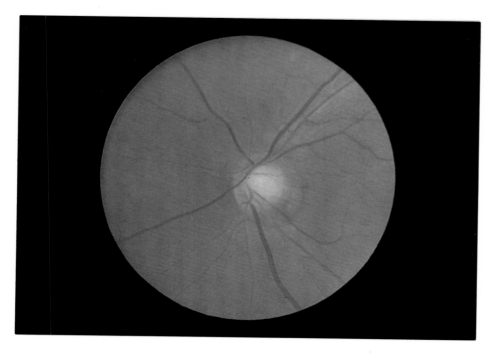

Fig. 4

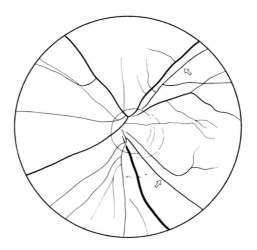

Generalized narrowing of the retinal arteriole
(of moderate grade)

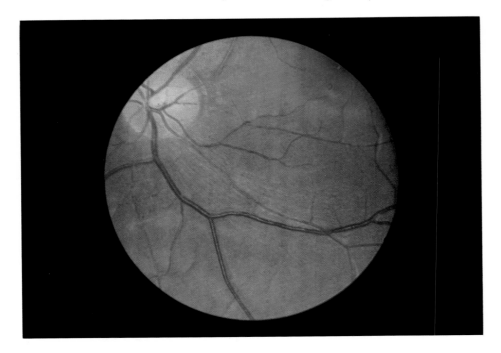

Fig. 5

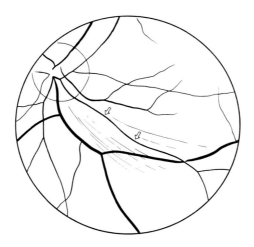

Arteriolar narrowing calibre-irregularity
(of moderate grade)

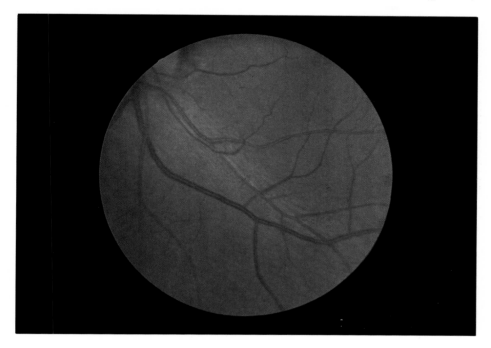

Fig. 6

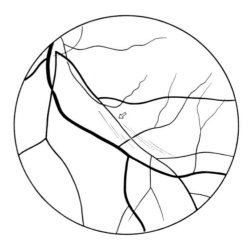

Localized narrowing of the retinal arteriole —arteriolar narrowing with calibre-irregularity (of slight grade)

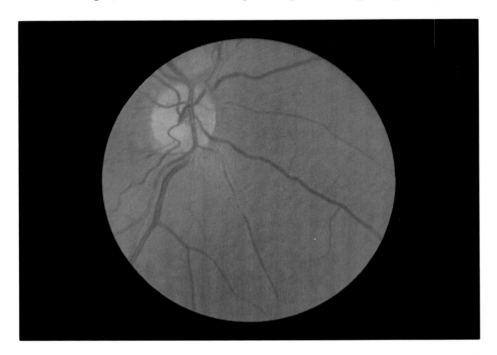

Fig. 7

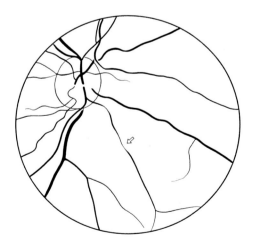

Segmental narrowing of the retinal arteriole —arteriolar narrowing with calibre-irregularity (of moderate grade)

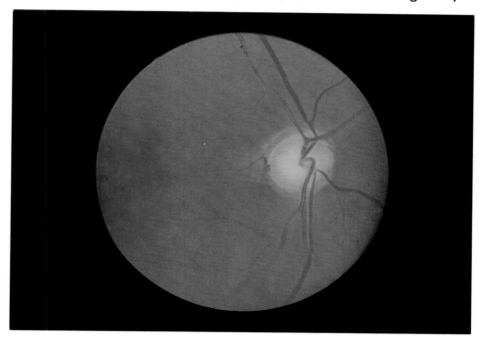

Fig. 8

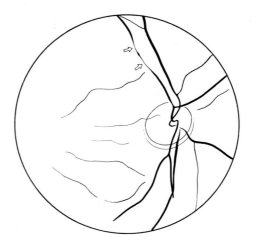

Organic narrowness (of slight grade)

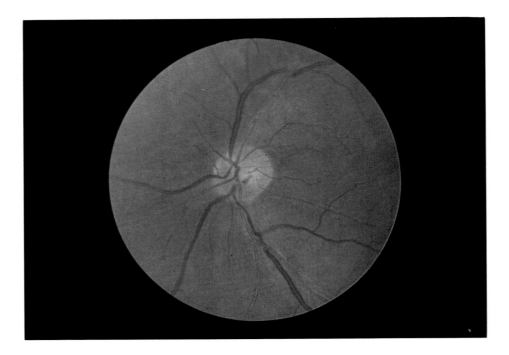

Fig. 9

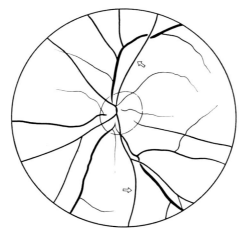

There are arteriovenous crossing signs, reflex-increases and slight indentations of the retinal arterioles also.

Organic narrowness (of moderate grade)

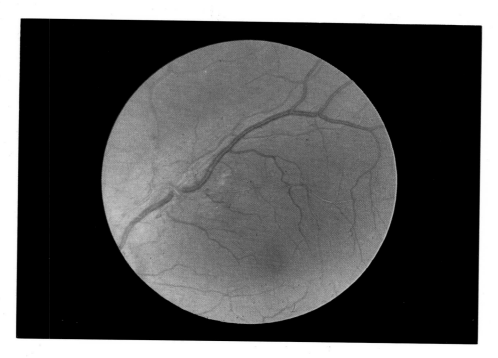

Fig. 10

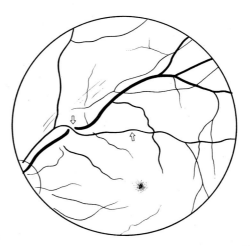

This is accompanied with arteriovenous crossing phenomenon and arteriolar reflex-increase of moderate grade.

Angiospastic narrowing (of moderate grade)

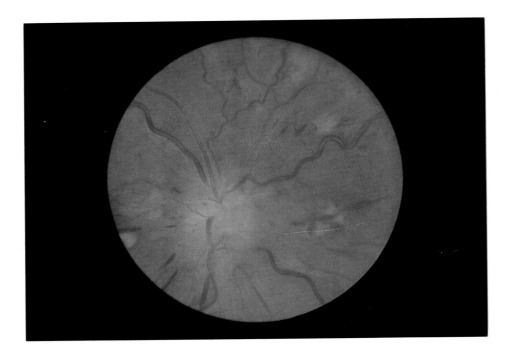

Fig. 11

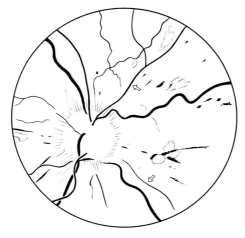

There are haemorrhages and white spots of the retina, oedema of the retina and optic disc accompanied with arteriolar narrowing.

Angiospastic narrowing (of severe grade)

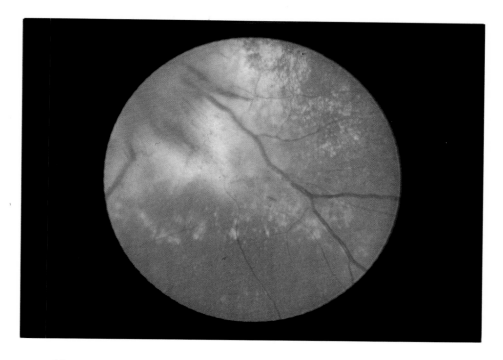

Fig. 12

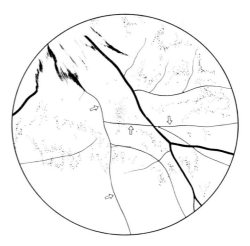

Marked narrowing of the retinal arteriole is accompanied by oedema of the optic disc and haemorrhages, and white spots of the retina.

Functional narrowing (a case of eclamptic toxaemia)

a. in ante-partum stage

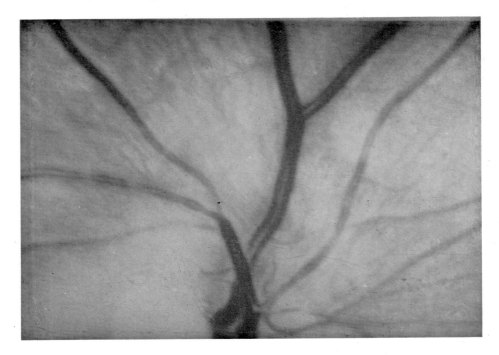

Fig. 13

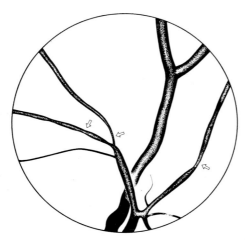

The arrows show localized narrowing of the retinal arterioles (of moderate grade).

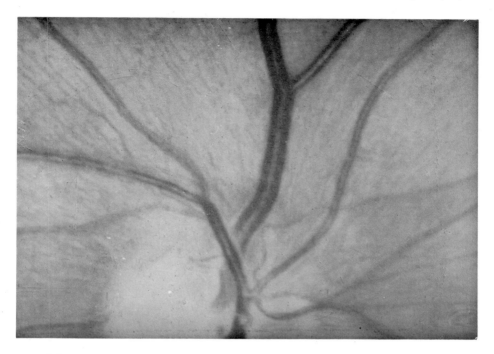

Fig. 14

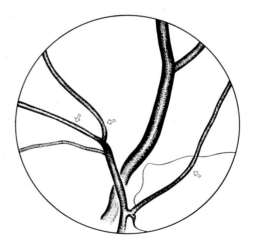

Disappearance of the localized
narrowing in ante-partum stage
are shown here.

Mixed type of arteriolar narrowing

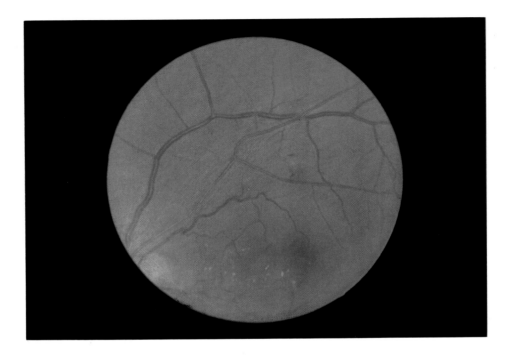

Fig. **15**

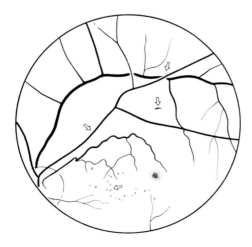

Arteriolar narrowing with arterio-venous crossing signs, small hae-morrhages, and white spots are shown.

Diffuse arteriolar narrowness in the fundus of a myopic eye

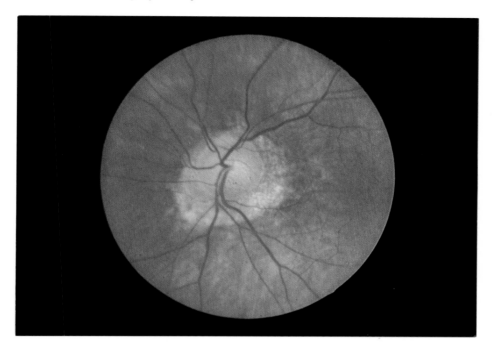

Fig. 16

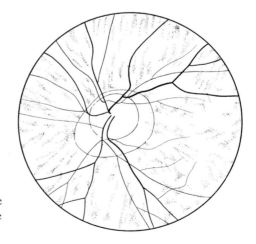

Though in the retinal arteriole diffuse narrowness is shown, the venules also appear to be narrow at the same time. Such fundus changes have no relation to hypertension.

Diffuse arteriolar narrowness in pigmentary degeneration of the retina

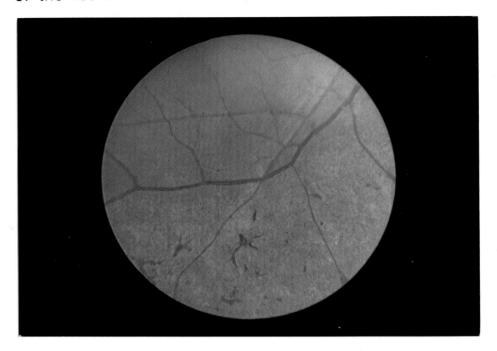

Fig. 17

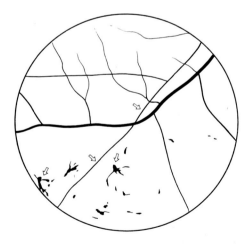

Though in the retinal arteriole diffuse narrowness is shown, one must notice black pigment spots and depigmented pigment spots.

Changes in reflex from the arteriolar wall
(Changes in the arteriolar light streaks)
··········Increase in reflex and opacification of the arteriolar wall
(Fig. 18~23)

Normal retinal arterioles appear bright rosy red in colour and in the middle of each arteriole runs a whitish bright reflex which is called a reflex streak or light streak.

When there is an increase in width and brightness of the reflex streak, if the contour of the reflex streak is distinct, the change is described as "increase in reflex streak"; if the contour is indistinct, the change is described as "opacification in the arteriolar wall".

1) Grading of increase in reflex-streak is made as follows in reference to the ratio AR/AC. The ratio AR/AC means the ratio of the width of the reflex streak (AR) to the width of the blood column of the arteriole (AC).

Assessment	Description	Ophthalmoscopic impression	AR/AC ratio
Normal	−	in normal limits	40~45%
Slight	+	slight increase	45~55%
Marked	++	marked increase	60% or more

(−)   (+)   (++)

40%   50%   60%

2) Description of changes in tone and intensity of the reflex streak. Colour tone and brightness of the reflex should be described.

For example;

reddish	light
yellowish	brilliant
whitish	copper-wired
	silver-wired
	white-lined
	dim
	etc.

If necessary, the site and extent of the change may be noted.

generalized
localized or focal
segmental or segmentary
irregular

Note : The ophthalmoscopical appearance of the reflex streak or opacification of the arteriolar wall is variable according to the condition of the retinal tissues, size of the pupil, and type and intensity of the light used in ophthalmoscopy, etc.

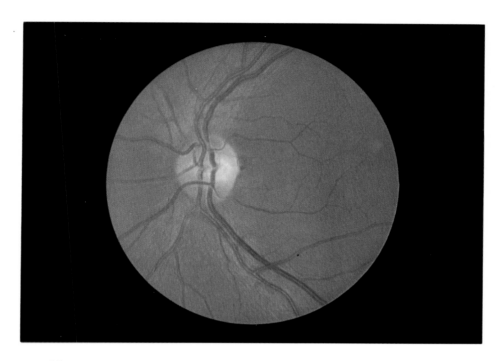

Fig. 18

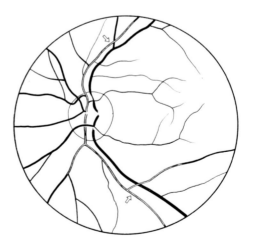

Reflex-increase of the retinal arteriole (of slight grade)

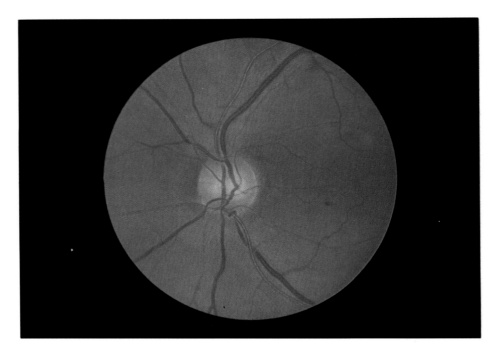

Fig. 19

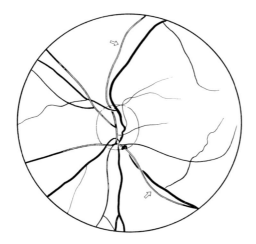

Increased arteriolar reflex (of slight grade)

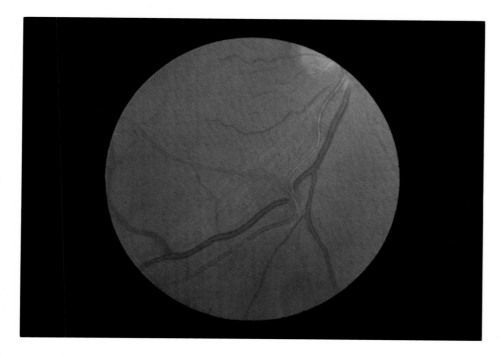

Fig. 20

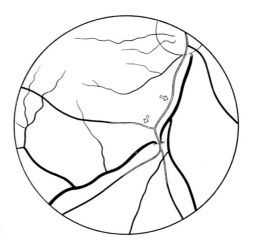

Colour-tone and brightness, like
copper-wired artery, and an arteriovenous crossing phenomenon
are shown.

Increase of the arteriolar reflex (of moderate grade)

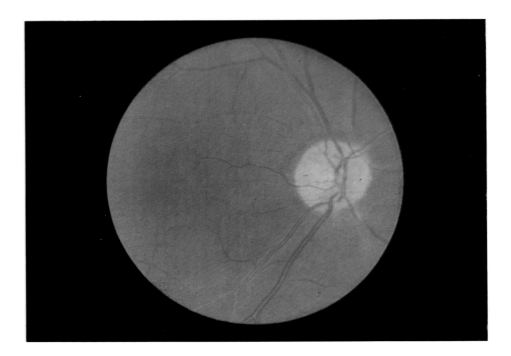

Fig. 21

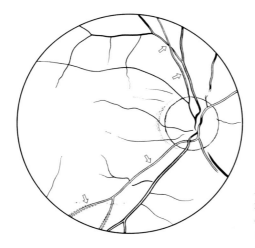

At a. temporalis superior et inferior the arteriolar reflex markedly increases and is surrounded. Partially with white sheathing considerable arterio-venous crossing phenomena, too, are found.

Increase of the arteriolar reflex (of moderate grade)

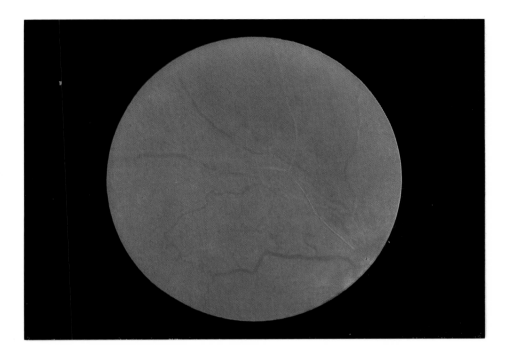

Fig. 22

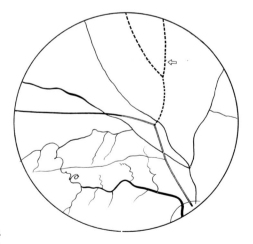

Like a silver-wired artery in its colour tone and brightness, it shows white lining at one part (indicated by a dotted line)

Increased arteriolar reflex (of moderate grade)

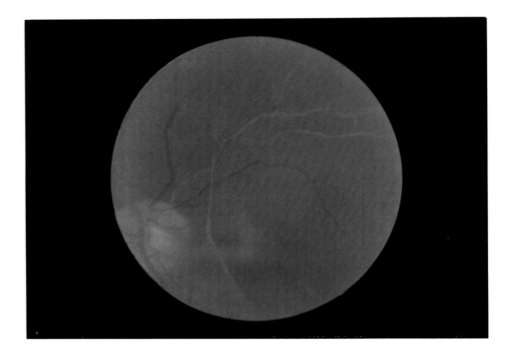

Fig. 23

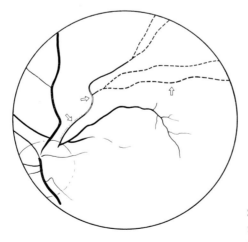

Some parts of the retinal arteriole, indicated by arrows, are increased reflex-stripe, and of these the dotted portions are "silver-wired".

Sheathing of the vessels

(Fig. 24~26)

Sheathing of the vessels is visible as a greyish white streak on either side of the blood column of the retinal vessels. This change varies in appearance between a faint one and a significant one and occurs not only locally but also diffusely.

Note :
1. Sheathing of vessels is observed sometimes as a congenital but non-pathologic change, particularly along the vessels in or near the optic disc.
2. Sheathing may also occur as a sequel of papillitis or many types of retinopathy, independent of hypertensive disease.

Sheathing of the arteriole

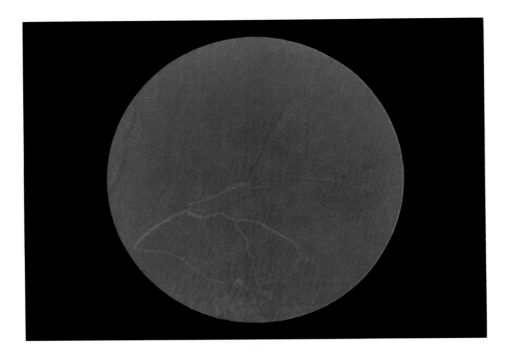

Fig. 24

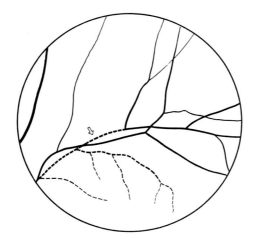

34

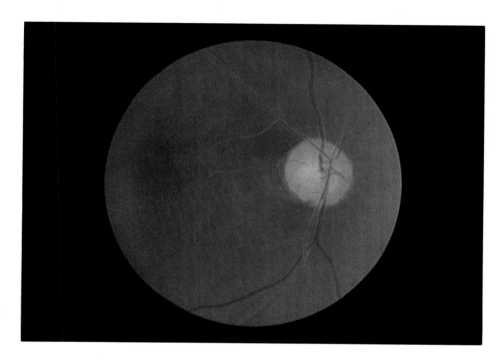

Fig. 25

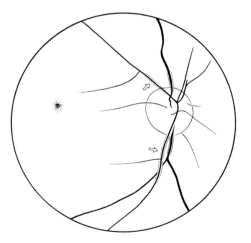

Sheathing of the arteriole

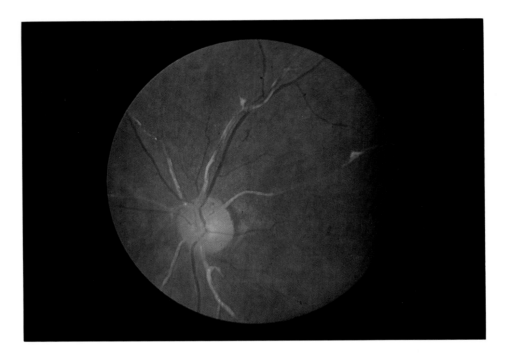

Fig. 26

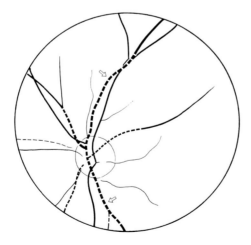

At the arterioles indicated by dotted lines marked sheathings are showed.

Perivascular stripe of the arterioles

(Fig. 27, 28)

This change is recognized as a kind of faint reflex or slight opacification in the retina along the arteriole but is less significant than sheathing of the vessels.

Perivascular stripe

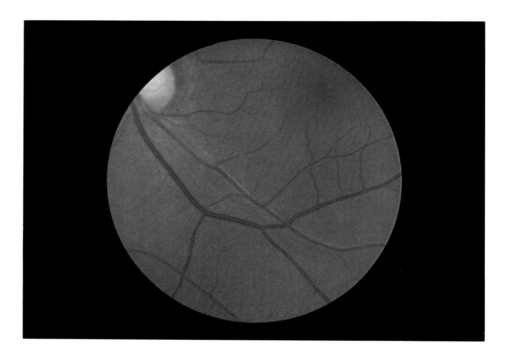

Fig. 27

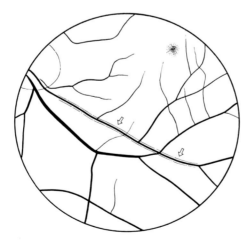

Perivascular stripe is shown as a whitish reflex along the inferior temporal artery.

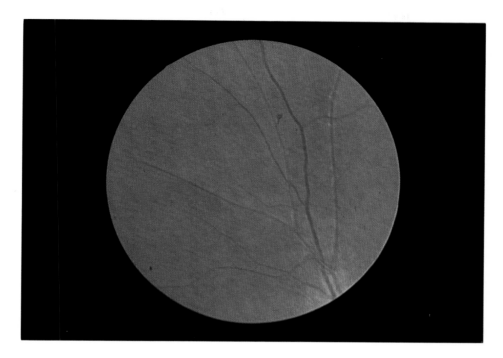

Fig. 28

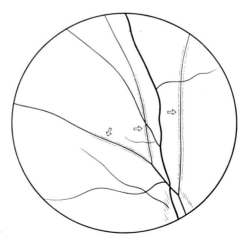

Perivascular stripes appear to be
whitish reflex along the arterioles, though they are somewhat
obscure compared with white
sheathing.

Changes in tortuosity of the vessels

The course of the central artery of the retina makes a serpentine curve of a certain tortuosity in the normal eye.

There are two types of changes in tortuosity: "Increase in tortuosity" and decrease in tortuosity, namely "straightening". If there is multiple localized straightening in a short course of the vessel, it may appear zig-zag.

The degree of tortuosity of the vessels is indicated by a ratio of the linear distance between two points on the course of a vessel to the actual distance measured along the course of the vessel between these two points by means of "kirubimeter".

In brief, it is possible to assess ophthalmoscopically the difference between the tortuosity of an arteriole and its accompanying venule.

The curve ratio

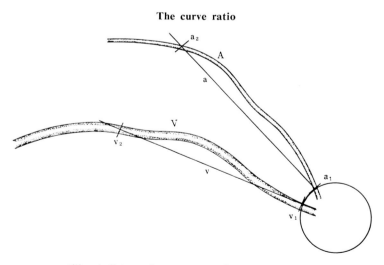

$a = a_1a_2$: rectilineal distance between a_1 and a_2.
A = curved distance measured by use of kirubimeter between a_1 and a_2.
$v = v_1v_2$: rectilineal distance between v_1 and v_2.
V = curved distance measured by use of kirubimeter between v_1 and v_2.

1) Straightening of the Arterioles (Fig. 29)

1. Extent and site of straightening of the arterioles must be described.
2. Grading and its assessment are made as following, according to the curve ratio :

Assessment	Description	Curve ratio (A/a)
Normal	−	1.020～1.035
Slight	+	1.015～1.020
Marked	‡	1.000～1.015

Note :
1. Peripheral branches and nasal branches of the arterioles are physiologically less tortuous than temporal ones.
2. Straightening of the arterioles is accompanied, mostly, with narrowing or calibre-irregularity.

2) Increase in Tortuosity of the Arterioles (Fig. 30, 31)

1. Extent and site of the abnormally tortuous arteriole must be described.
2. Grading and its assessment are made as follows, according to the curve ratio.

Assessment	Description	Curve ratio (A/a)
Normal	−	1.020～1.035
Slight	+	1.035～1.050
Marked	‡	1.055～1.085

Note :
1. There may be congenital variation.
2. When capillary and pre- or postcapillary arterioles become tortuous, they appear corkscrew-shaped, such as that seen under a state of peristatic hyperaemia or so-called "vermehrte Kapillarenzeichnung".
3. Although increased tortuosity of the large retinal arterioles is a sign of arteriolar sclerosis, it may be observed very often in young patients in an early stage of hypertension.

3) Increase in Tortuosity of the Venules (Fig. 32, 33)

1. Extent and site of the change must be described.
2. Grading and its assessment are made as in the case of arterioles, according to the curve ratio (V/v).

Note :
1. There may be congenital variation to some extent.
2. Corkscrew-shaped tortuosity of the small venules and pre- and postcapillaries in the macular region can be named as "Guist's phenomenon".
3. Tortuosity of the venules may be observed also in cases of heart failure or hypotension, independent of hypertensive disease.

Straightening of the arteriole

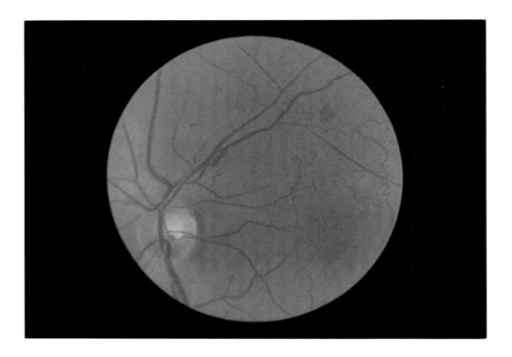

Fig. 29

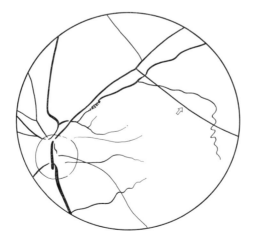

Increase in tortuosity of the arteriole
(of moderate grade)

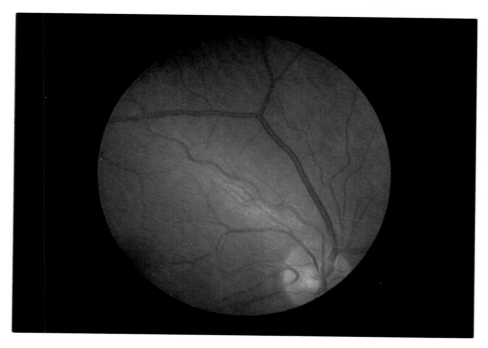

Fig. 30

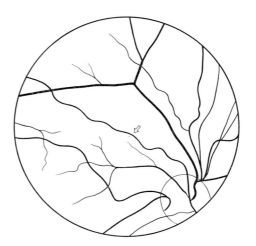

Increase in tortuosity of the arteriole
(of moderate grade)

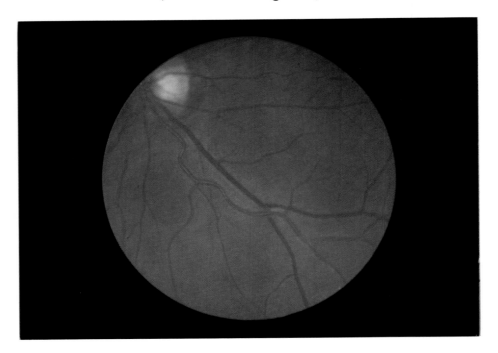

Fig. 31

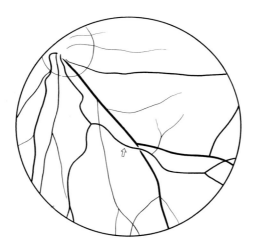

Increase in tortuosity of the venule
(of slight grade)

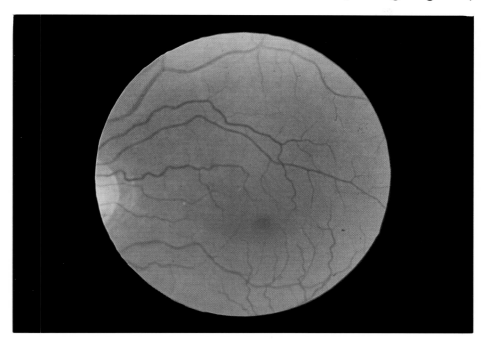

Fig. 32

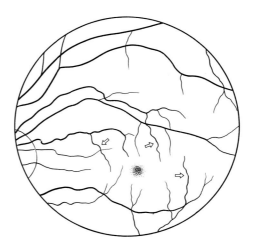

Increase in tortuosity of the venule (of moderate grade)

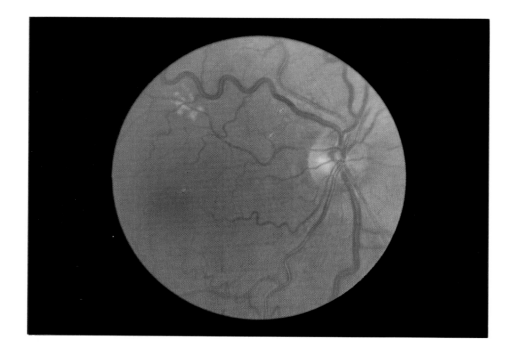

Fig. 33

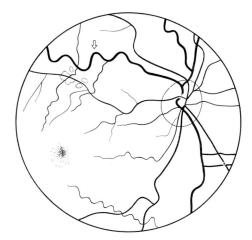

This picture shows remarkable dilatation and tortuosity of the venules.

Branching angles of the retinal arterioles

(Fig. 34, 35)

As the central retinal artery emerges from the optic disc and ranges to the peripheral area, ramifying its branches, the angle made by the two bifurcated arteries is called the branching angle.

Method of measurement: Measurement of the branching angle is carried out by means of fundus photograph, and the method of measurement and location (for example, the 1st branch of the temporal superior artery) are described.

1) When tangent lines are drawn, abutting the inside of the two vessels bifurcating from the branching point of the retinal vessel, the angle thus formed is measured.

2) When points on the central lines of two vessels parted from the bifurcated region at a certain distance (0.5-0.1 P. D., that is, 0.5 P. D. on the trunk artery, and 0.1 P. D. on the peripheral artery, are adequate) are dotted, the angle between them and the branched point is determined.

Standard for determination
First bifurcation of the temporal superior artery   73.1° ($\sigma=18.0$)
Bifurcation of the precapillary artery leading to the macula
                                           86.9° ($\sigma=19.1$)

Note:
    In measuring, a fundus photograph in which the branching region is filmed near the center of the scene should be adopted if possible.

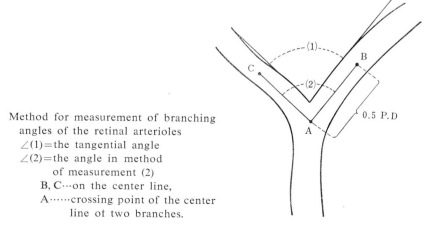

Method for measurement of branching
  angles of the retinal arterioles
    ∠(1)=the tangential angle
    ∠(2)=the angle in method
        of measurement (2)
     B, C···on the center line,
      A······crossing point of the center
        line of two branches.

47

Abnormality of the branching angle

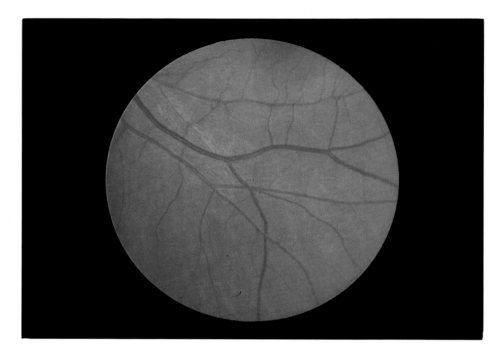

Fig. 34

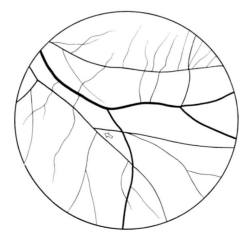

This picture shows acute-angled abnormality of the arteriole.

Abnormality of the branching angle

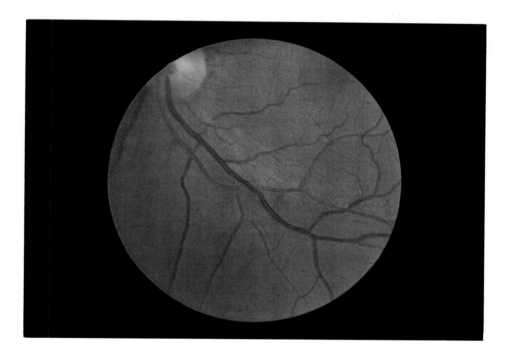

Fig. 35

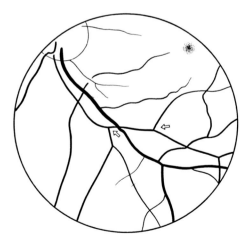

This picture shows obtuse-angled
abnormality of the arteriole.

Arterio-venous crossing phenomenon (Fig. 36~49)

The arterio-venous crossing phenomenon is a situation in which pathological findings of the venous blood column, such as abnormalities in appearance, calibre and course, are observed at the crossing sites.

The main pathological findings are as follows:

1) Tapering of the vein

The underlying vein appears tapered with its tip towards the artery at both sides of the crossing. Rarely, this occurs at one side of the crossing.

2) Banking of the vein

The underlying vein appears dilated for some length at the distal side of the crossing. Banking associated with concealment and tapering is sometimes called Gunn's sign.

3) Concealment of the vein

The blood column of the underlying vein appears interrupted for some width at the site of crossing.

4) Nicking of the vein

The blood column in the underlying vein appears constricted slightly at the crossing.

5) Humping of the vein

The blood column in the vein forms an upward hump when it crosses over the artery.

6) Inverse crossing phenomenon

The blood column in the overlying vein shows abnormal findings such as humping, localized narrowing, opacity, etc. at the crossing.

7) Depression of the vein

The underlying vein dips into the deeper retinal layers at the crossing.

8) Right-angled crossing

The underlying vein crosses the artery at a right angle only near the crossing. According to the shapes of courses of the veins, they are called S-, Z- or U-shaped right-angled crossing. U-shaped crossing

50

accompanied by tapering and/or concealment of the vein is sometimes called Salus' crossing arc.

9) Deviation of the vein

The blood column in the underlying vein deviates slightly at the crossing.

10) Parallel-Gunn's sign

The vein running parallel to the artery appears narrowed or interrupted when it approaches the artery.

Standards for judgment of the grades of arterio-venous crossing phenomena

1. A method of judgment

Using a schematic picture drawn as a standard of diagnosis, the grades are classified as follows: Non-diagnostic (N), Normal (−), Slight (+), Moderate (╫), Severe (╫╫), Special type of severe grade (╫╫').

2. Preconditions for judgment.

Findings within half of one disc diameter are disregarded. If there exist differences in grade of the findings in the same fundus or in both fundi, the decision should be made on the basis of the more severe ones. In evaluation of crossing phenomena, opacifications of the vascular wall, such as tapering and concealment, are made more accurately by photographs, but care should be taken not to mistake "out-of-focus" for opacification findings.

Judgment should be made at crossing sites where artery and vein show the normal calibre ratio of 2 to 3. If there is an abnormal difference in calibre between artery and vein, and there is no suitable crossing site for judgment, crossing can be used for judgment only when the artery is narrower than the vein, or in the reverse situation, only when the calibre ratio is below 1 to 3.

Suitable sites for evaluation lie between the first and the third division.

A distinct finding can be judged as it is, regardless of other conditions. But in the following cases, a judgment can be made with less positive findings:

Note:
When there is no suitable crossing site or in case of out-of-focus photographs, the evaluation should be "non-diagnostic (N).
  a) crossing phenomena with crossing angles below 30.
  b) crossing phenomena which occur near and distal from the bifurcation of the artery.
  c) crossing phenomena with retinal changes around crossed area.

Schemata for determination of the grade of arterio-venous crossing signs
(KATOH-MATSUI 1967)

slight grade   moderate grade   severe grade   special type of severe grade

1. Slight constriction at the crossed part.
2. Slight opacification (turbidity) of the site bordered by the artery.
3. Bow-shaped right-angled crossing (without calibre-variation of the vein).
4. Tapering of the vein at both sides of the artery which touches not at one point but along some length.
5. Band-shaped concealment of an obliquely crossed artery-vein.(Note differentiation from tapering of a high grade).
6. Bow-shaped right-angled crossing and slight tapering(Salussche Kreuzungsbogen).
7. Generally recognized concealment.
8. Tapering of the vein at both sides. (Remarkably thin contact with the artery).
9. Tapering and concealment of the vein.
10. Bow-shaped right-angled crossing, tapering and concealment.
11. One side of the crossed artery having a state similar to figure 4 and its other side having tapering and concealment.
12. One side of the crossed artery having a state to figure 7 and its other side having tapering and concealment.
13. Inverse crossing phenomenon.
14. Concealment and banking of the both sides.
15. Parallel-Gunn's phenomenon.

Note :

1. If there exist inadequate arterio-venous crossing or the photograph is badly out of focus, it should be labelled "impossible to judge", thus avoiding unnecessary work.
2. In judgment of the arterio-venous crossing phenomenon, the observer must attach most importance to the opacification of blood-vessel-walls.

Arterio-venous crossing phenomenon (of slight grade)

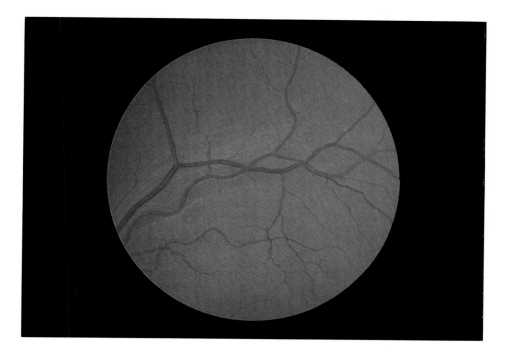

Fig. 36

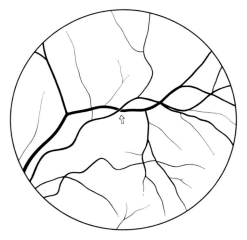

The arrow indicated slight constriction and opacification at the crossed part.

Arterio-venous crossing phenomenon (of slight grade)

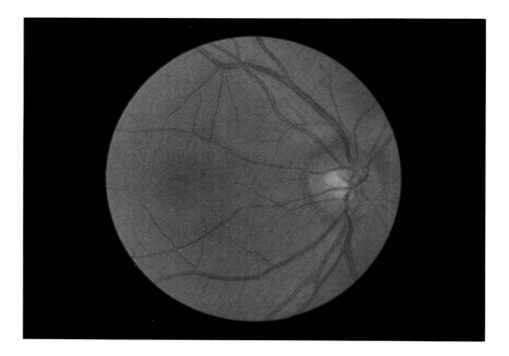

Fig. 37

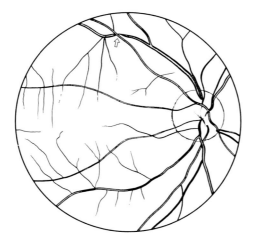

Arterio-venous crossing phenomenon (of moderate grade)

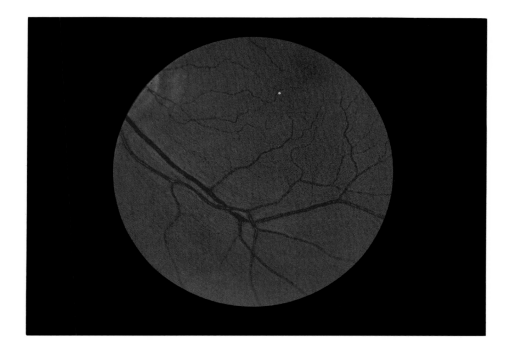

Fig. 38

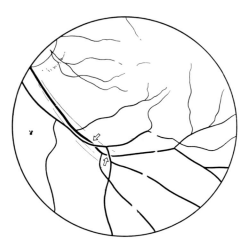

The arrows indicate slight tapering of the vein and bow-shaped
right-angled crossing.

Arterio-venous crossing phenomenon
(of moderate grade)

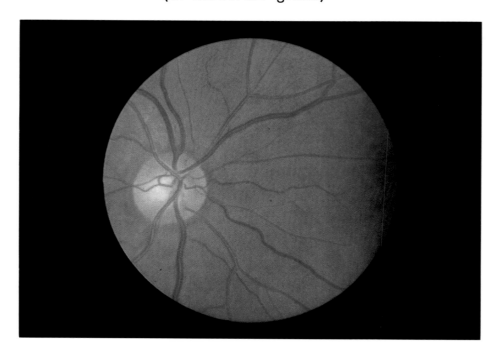

Fig. 39

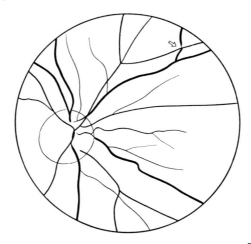

This picture indicates clearly a
bow-shaped right-angled crossing
with slight tapering.

Arterio-venous crossing phenomenon
(of moderate grade)

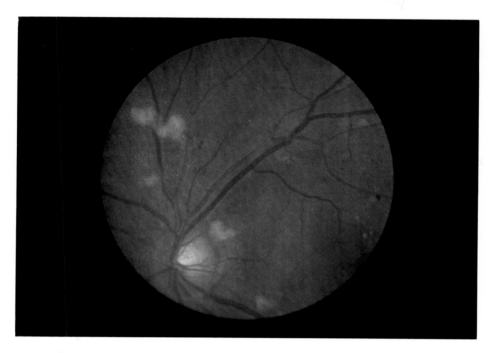

Fig. 40

This picture indicates a bow-shaped right-angled crossing.

Arterio-venous crossing phenomenon (of severe grade)

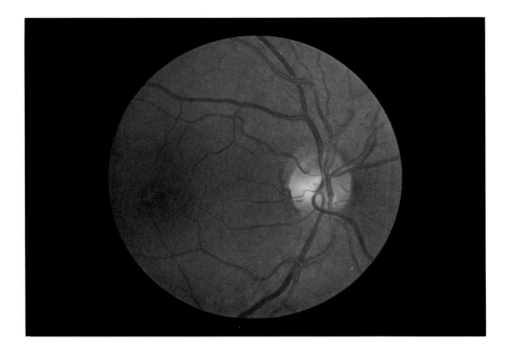

Fig. 41

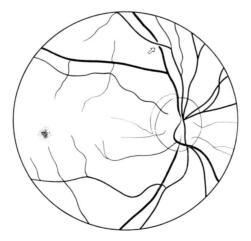

This figure shows typical tapering of the vein.

Arterio-venous crossing phenomenon (of severe grade)

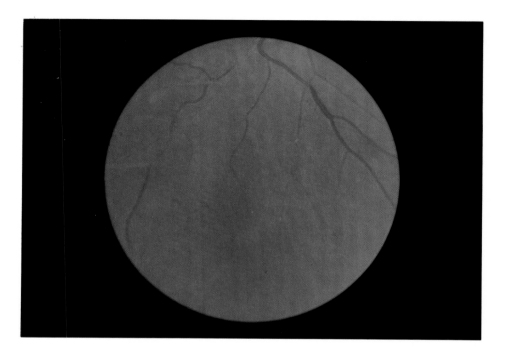

Fig. 42

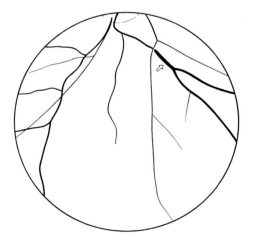

This figure shows typical banking of the vein.

Arterio-venous crossing phenomenon (of severe grade)

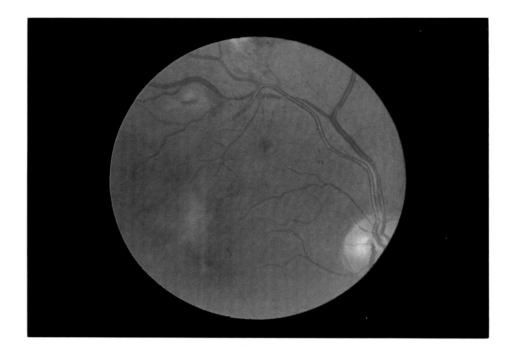

Fig. 43

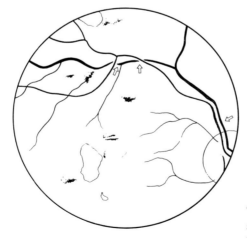

This picture indicated banking and tapering of the vein along V. temporalis superior, and near the optic disc a pararell-Gunn's phenomenon. *pararell*

Arterio-venous crossing phenomenon (of severe grade)

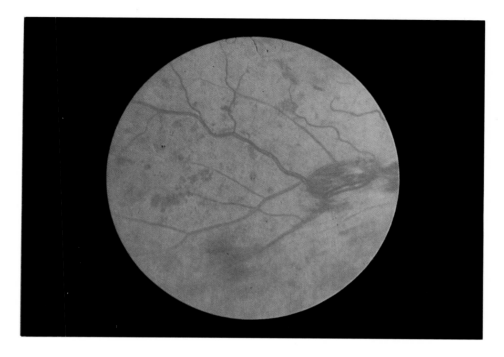

Fig. 44

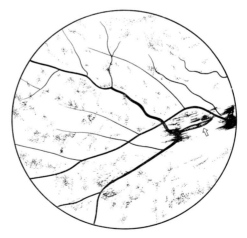

This picture indicated banking of the vein (impending obstruction).

Arterio-venous crossing phenomenon
(special type of severe grade)

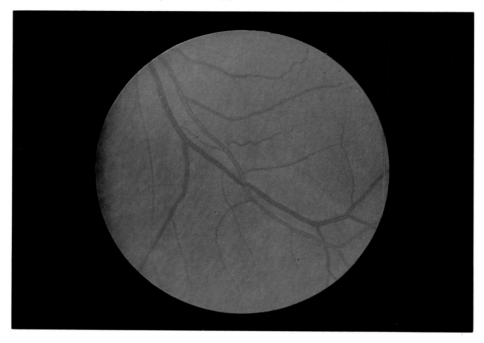

Fig. 45

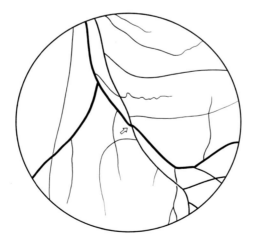

This figure shows inverse crossing phenomenon.

Arterio-venous crossing phenomenon (of slight grade)

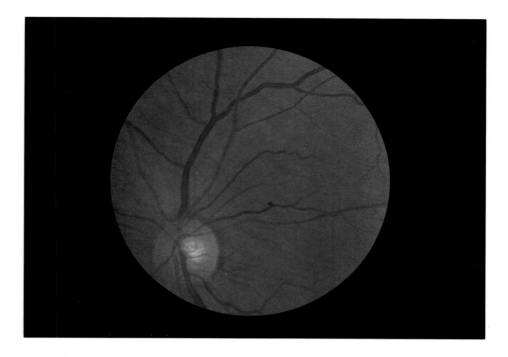

Fig. 46

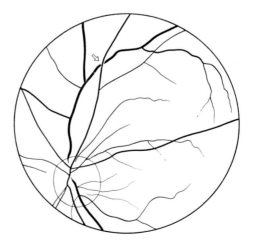

This picture shows deviation of
the vein.

Arterio-venous crossing phenomenon (of slight grade)

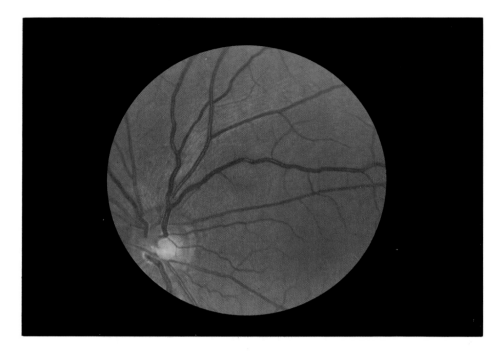

Fig. 47

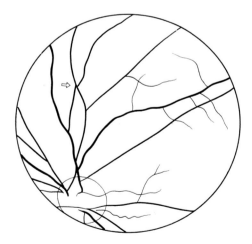

This picture shows deflection of the vein.

Arterio-venous crossing phenomenon
(special type of severe grade)

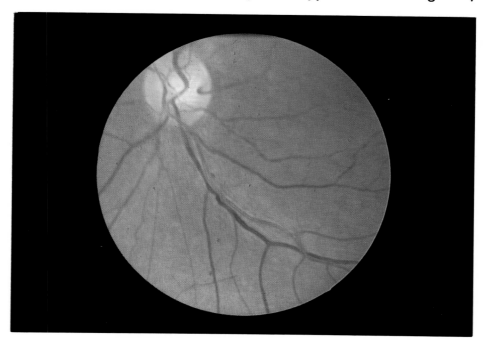

Fig. 48

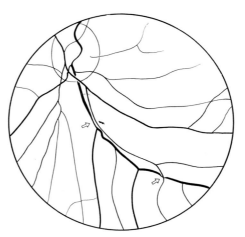

The arrows point to pararell-
Gunn's phenomenon and tapering
of the vein.

Arterio-venous crossing phenomenon
(of moderate grade)

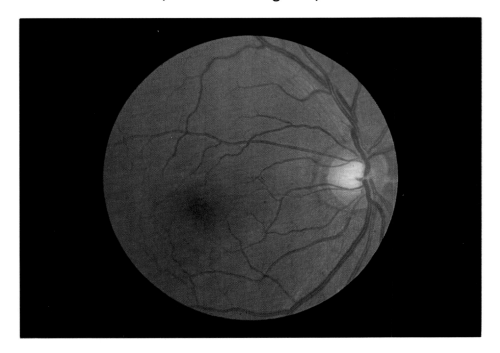

Fig. 49

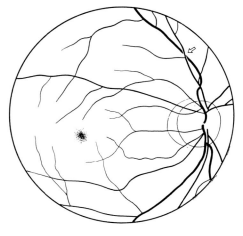

Band-shaped concealment of the
obliquely crossed artery-vein.
The crossing part near the optic
disc is ruled out from judgment

Fundus haemorrhages
(not including obstruction of the retinal vein)

Haemorrhages are classified as follows :
1) Retinal Haemorrhage (Fig. 50~52)
Striated haemorrhage, flame-shaped haemorrhage—Haemorrhages in the nerve fibre layer usually show these types of haemorrhage.

Punctiform haemorrhage—Haemorrhages in the inner and outer nuclear layer, and outer plexiform layer usually show this type of haemorrhage.

Fleck-shaped haemorrhage—Massive haemorrhages in the inner and outer nuclear layer, and outer plexiform layer usually show this type of haemorrhage.

2) Choroidal Haemorrhage (Fig. 53)
Dark red, and usually round or fleck-shaped.

3) Preretinal Haemorrhage (Fig. 54)
Retinal haemorrhage which had leaked under the internal limiting membrane or subhyaloid space. After a period of time the red blood corpuscles sink and the haemorrhage appears keel-shaped with a straight upper margin.

4) Vitreous Haemorrhage (Fig. 55)
This is haemorrhage which has flowed into the vitreous from the retina or preretinal space, or haemorrhage from new vessels in the vitreous. They appear striated, drop-like, thread-like or mass-like. After a period of time, they are organized and become yellowish-white and have a tendency to sink in the vitreous. It is desirable to describe the site of the haemorrhage (by quadrant) and the size and number of haemorrhages for reference.

Note:
Differential diagnosis between micro-aneurysm and punctiform haemorrhage is sometimes difficult with routine ophthalmoscopic examination or fundus photographs.

Retinal haemorrhage

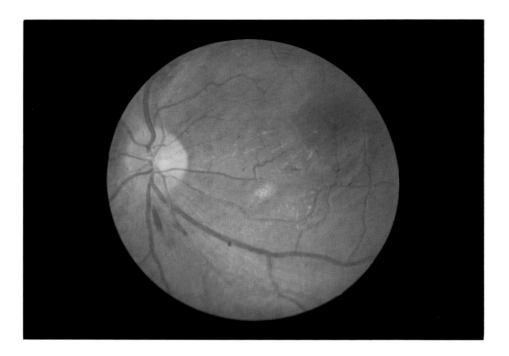

Fig. 50

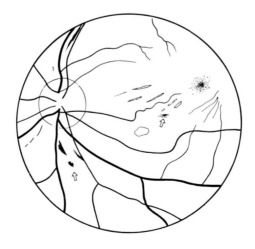

Punctiforme haemorrhage and striated haemorrhage are shown.

Retinal haemorrhage

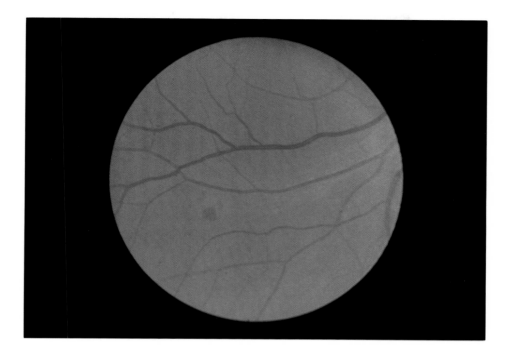

Fig. 51

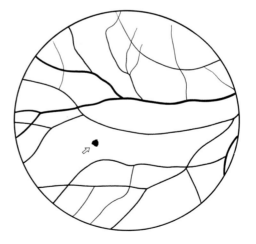

Small fleck-shaped haemorrhage
is showed.

Retinal haemorrhage

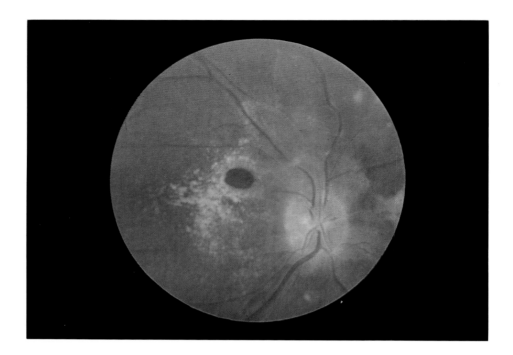

Fig. 52

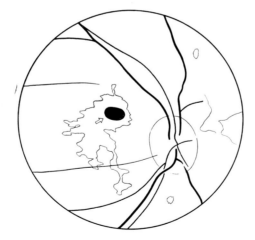

Fleck-shaped haemorrhage is showed.

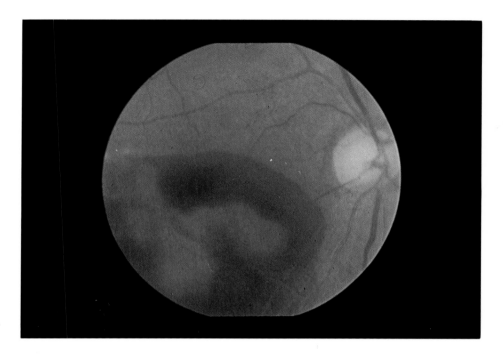

Fig. 53

Preretinal haemorrhage

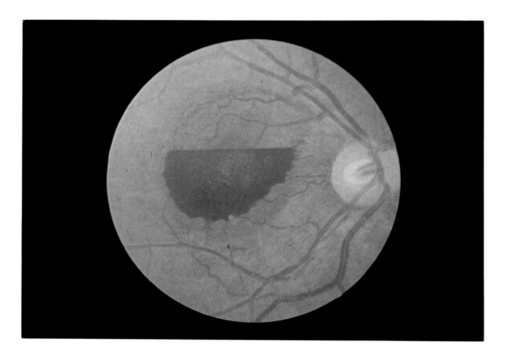

Fig. 54

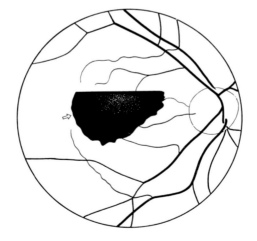

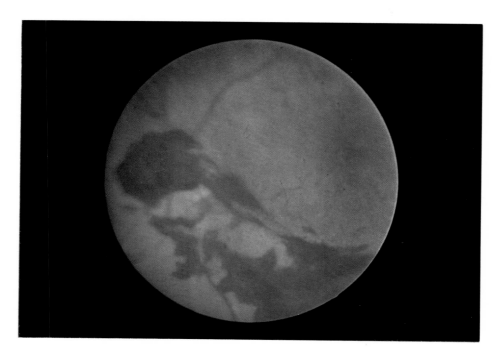

Fig. 55

White spots in the retina (Fig. 56~60)

White spots are divided into hard spots and soft spots. Hard white spots appear white or grayish white with distinct margins, and seem to stick to the retina. Their sizes range from powder-like to one fourth of a disc diameter. Some of them appear after the oedema or haemorrhage has been absorbed; others are masses of exudates, degenerative foci, etc. Star-figures are usually thought to be formed of hard white spots and occur frequently in cases of hypertension or renal diseases but are not specific for these diseases.

Soft white spots are usually larger than hard ones and have ill-defined margins like pieces of cotton which appear to float on the supperficial retinal layer. Cotton wool patches are typical soft white spots.

Note (Fig. 61~64):
> Care should be taken in differentiating white patches seen in cases of obstruction of the vein, from drusen and medullated nerve fibres.

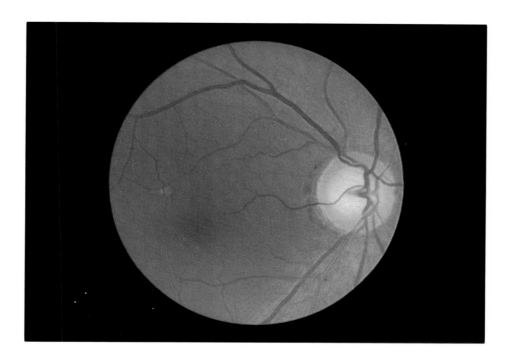

Fig. 56

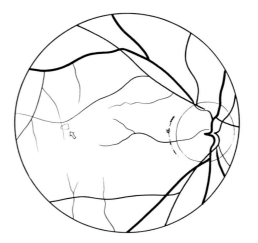

Hard white spots

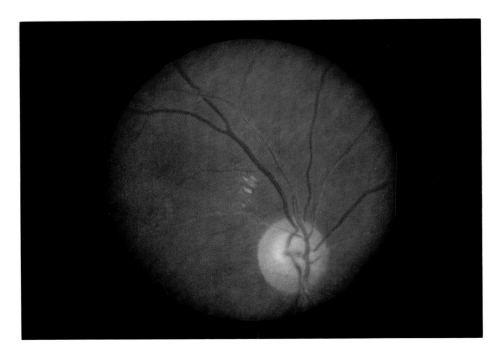

Fig. 57

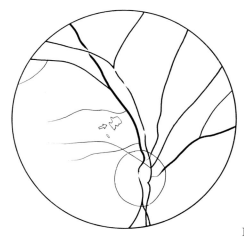

In this picture calibre-irregularity of the arteriole and arterio-venous crossing phenomenon too are seen.

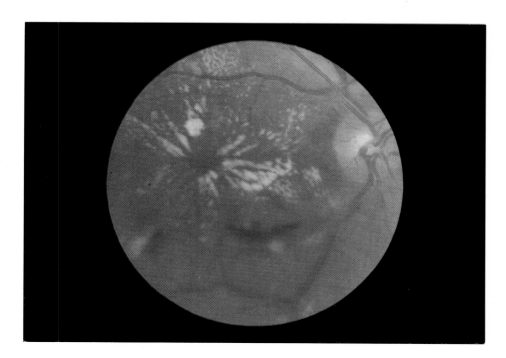

Fig. 58

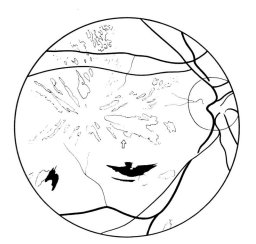

Soft white spots

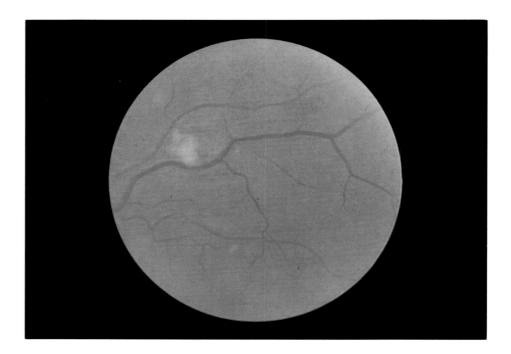

Fig. 59

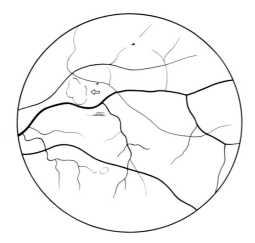

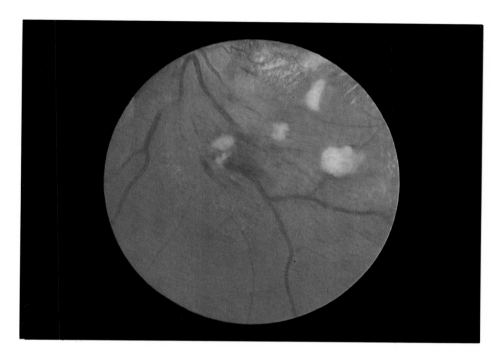

Fig. 60

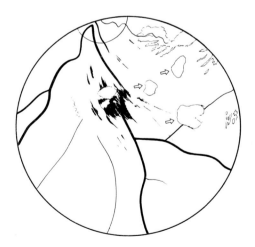

White patches found in obstruction of the central retinal vein

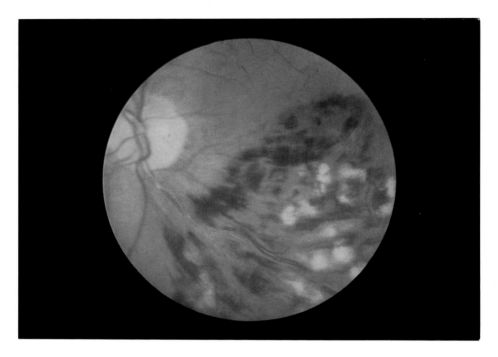

Fig. 61

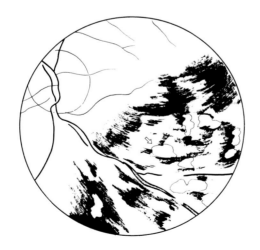

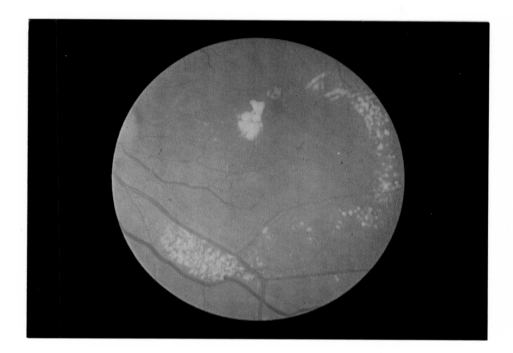

Fig. 62

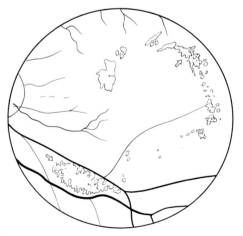

These white patches appeared
after absorption of haemorrhages
found in obstruction of the retinal vein.

Druse

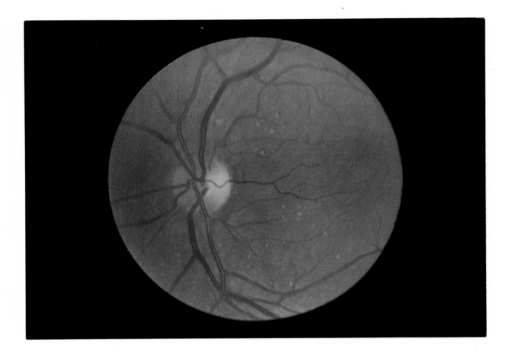

Fig. 63

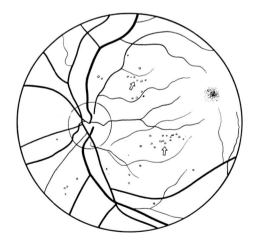

Drusen should be differentiated from white patches.

Medullated nerve fibre

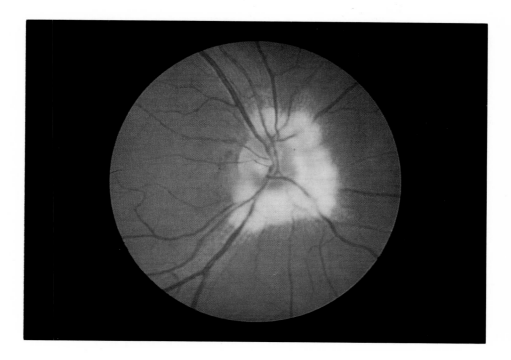

Fig. 64

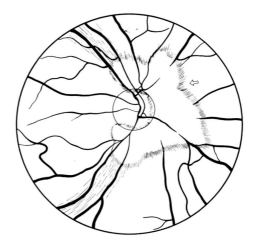

Venous obstruction

In obstruction of the central vein, haemorrhages are seen scattered radially from the optic disc in every directions. In obstruction of a branch of the retinal vein, the haemorrhage appears fan-shaped with its apex at the site of the obstruction.

1) Obstruction of the Central Retinal Vein (Fig. 65~68)
This is classified as follows according to the grades of haemorrhage :
  i) Haemorrhage of slight grade : Striated, punctiform, or small fleck-shaped scattered haemorrhages (impending obstruction).
  ii) Haemorrhage of moderate grade : Though the haemorrhage is massive, the retina can be seen at places through it.
  iii) Haemorrhage of severe grade : because of massive haemorrhages, the retina can not be seen through them.
2) Obstruction of a Branch of the Retinal Vein (Fig. 69~71)
  i) The grades of haemorrhage are classified according to the same standard as in the case of obstruction of the central vein.
  ii) The sites of obstruction are classified as follows :
        superior (inferior) lateral region
        superior (inferior) internal region
        superior (inferior) papillary vein

Impending obstruction of the central retinal vein

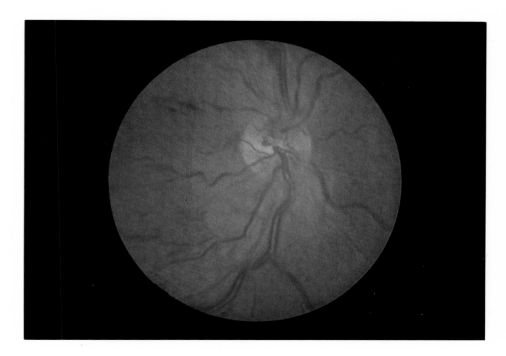

Fig. 65

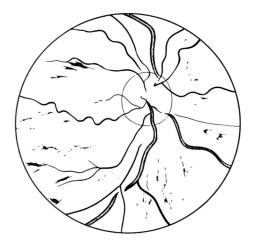

Obstruction of the central retinal vein

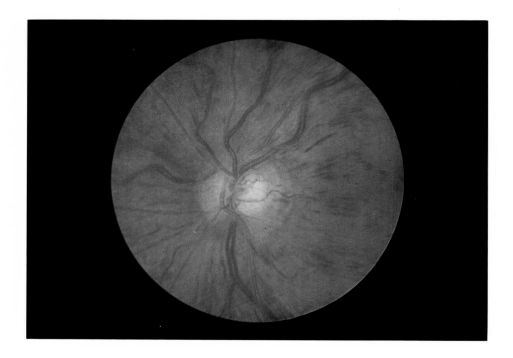

Fig. 66

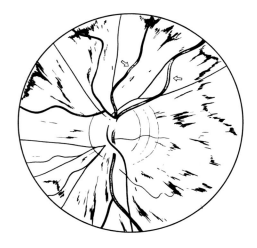

Haemorrhages of slight grade.

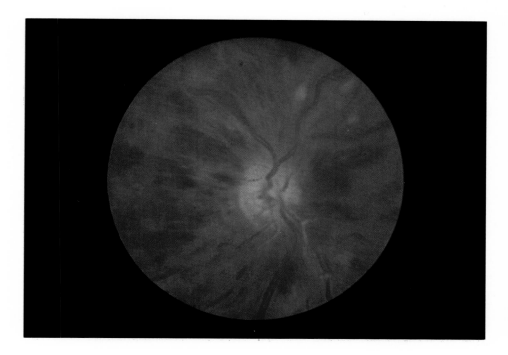

Fig. 67

Haemorrhages of moderate grade.

Obstruction of the central retinal vein

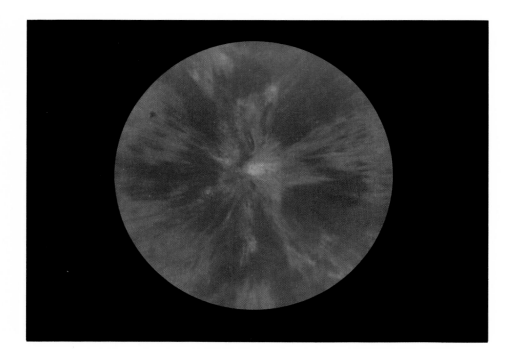

Fig. 68

Haemorrhages of severe grade.

Branch-obstruction of the central retinal vein

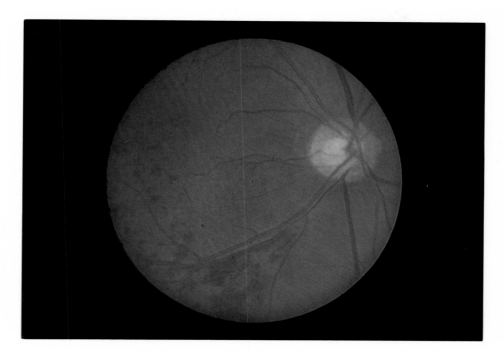

Fig. 69

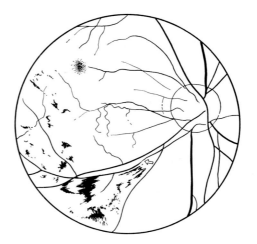

Haemorrhages of slight grade.

Branch-obstruction of the central retinal vein

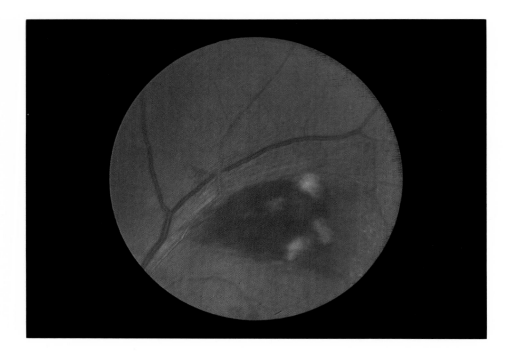

Fig. 70

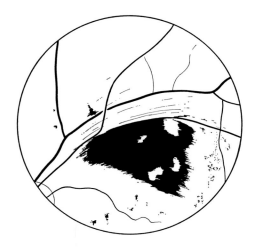

Haemorrhages of severe grade.

Impending obstruction of a branch of central retinal vein

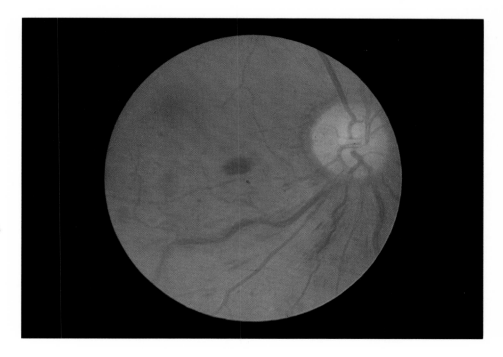

Fig. 71

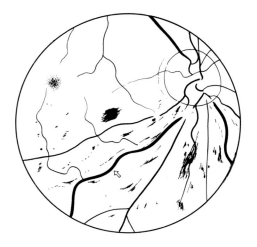

A case of slight haemorrhage.

Neovascularization in the retina (Fig. 72~74)

This sometimes means new growth of the retinal vessels. Here it means, however, a case in which the retinal and preretinal capillaries came to be observed more markedly with the ophthalmoscope than usual as a result of their dilatation.

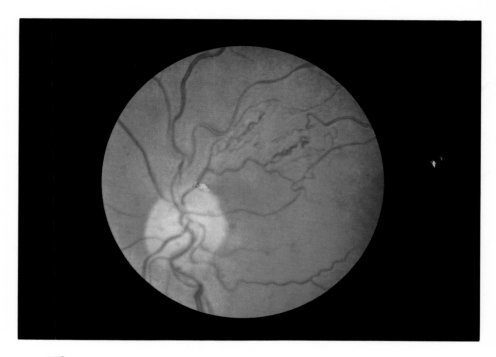

Fig. 72

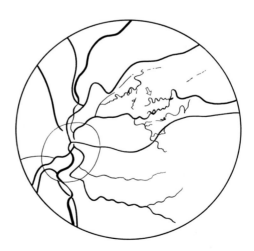

Neovascularization in the retina

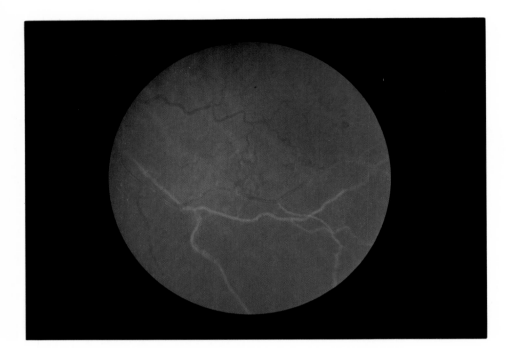

Fig. 73

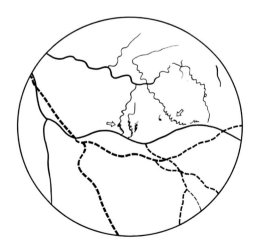

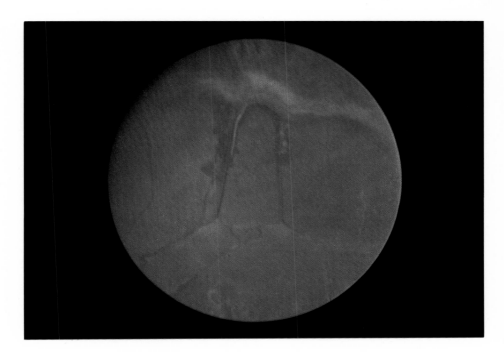

Fig. 74

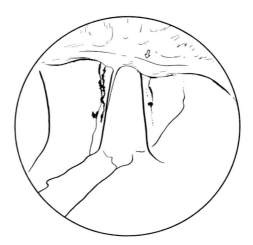

Neovascularization in the vitreous (Fig. 75)

This is a case in which new growth of vessels is seen in the vitreous. Blood vessels are derived from disc or retinal vessels and are
usually associated with new proliferative tissues.

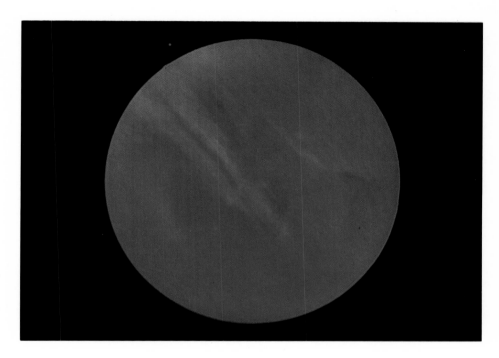

Fig. 75

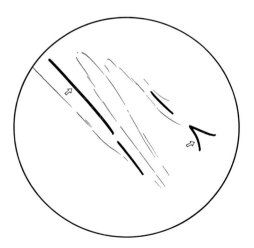

Anastomosis of the retinal vessels (Fig. 76, 77)

One or two new vessels have dilated markedly and have become connected with two preexisting retinal vessels. Sometimes two vessels make anastomoses at two points of one vessel.

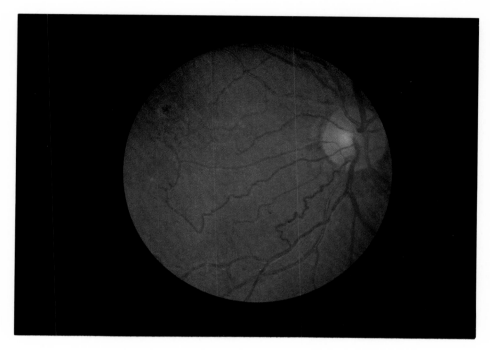

Fig. 76

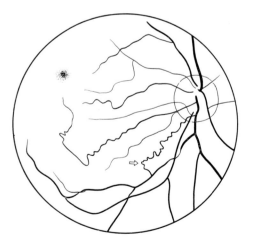

Anastomosis of the retinal vessels

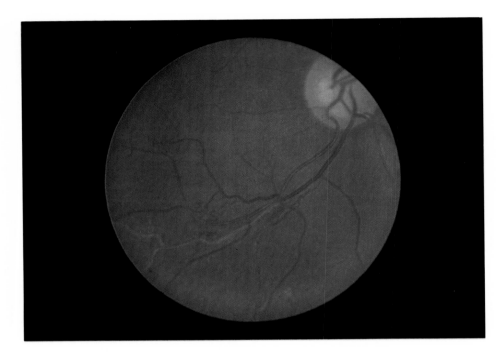

Fig. 77

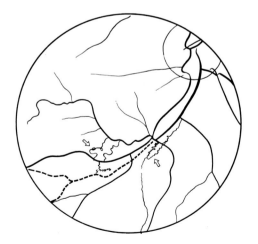

Proliferated tissues

(Fig. 78, 79)

They are seen as white, grayish-white or yellowish-white and opaque, striated or membranous proliferated tissues on the surface of the retina or in the vitreous.

Proliferated tissues in the retina and vitreous

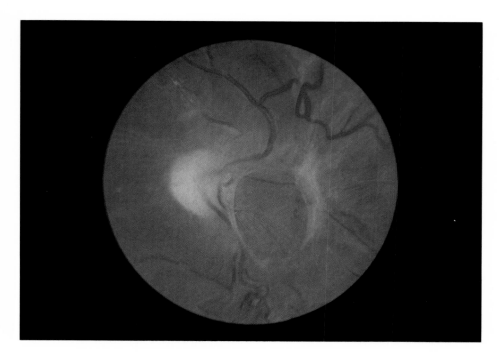

Fig. 78

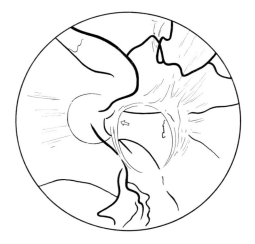

Proliferated tissues near the optic disc

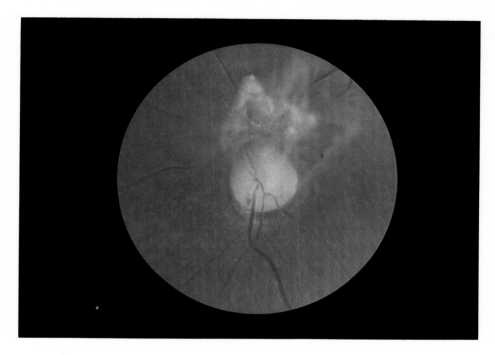

Fig. 79

Changes of the optic disc

1) Pallor of the Disc (Fig. 80)

The optic disc appears pale. This is observed in various conditions. This is also observed in cases of hypertensive diseases such as chronic nephritis, etc., and is usually associated with anaemia.

2) Optic Atrophy (Fig. 81, 82)

This is a condition in which nerve fibres of the optic trunk have degenerated. The optic disc is pathologically pale. Decrease in visual acuity and defects in the visual field are present. This is an irreversible condition both functionally and organically.

3) Papilloedema (Fig. 83, 84)

This is an oedema of the optic disc due to circulatory disturbances. The optic disc is elevated and its margin is indistinct. The difference of height between the face of the optic disc and the macula is measured with an ophthalmoscope and its difference is expressed in diopters. Sometimes papilloedema means a case with a difference in height of more than 2 D. Generally the central visual acuity is rather good for its fundus picture, but decreases in the last stage.

In the very early stage the optic disc is oedematous and transparent but, as time goes on, hyperaemia, swelling, congestion and tortuosity of the vessels become marked. In the advanced stage haemorrhages and white spots appear in the retina. After a long period of time, secondary inflammatory changes and further secondary atrophy of the optic disc are induced. Visual acuity is decreased and the colour of the optic disc becomes grayish white.

Note (Fig. 85):
Papilloedema is caused by various diseases such as optic neuritis, papillitis, pseudoneuritis, and brain tumor. Care should be taken in differential diagnosis of the underlying disease.

104

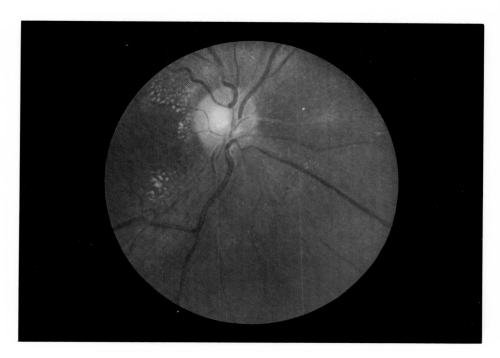

Fig. 80

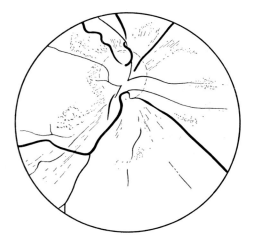

The optic disc appears to be pale, but vision is normal.

Optic atrophy

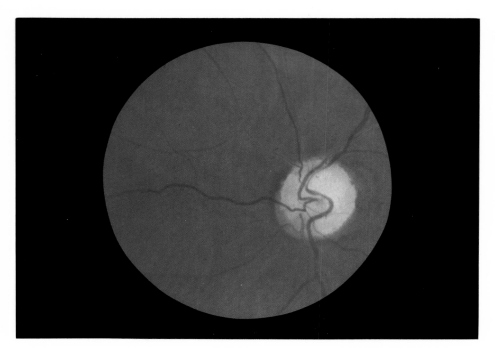

Fig. 81

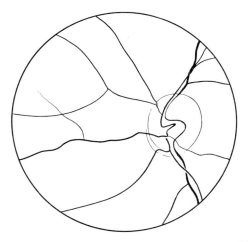

The number of capillaries over the optic disc have decreased markedly (2/normal 6-7).

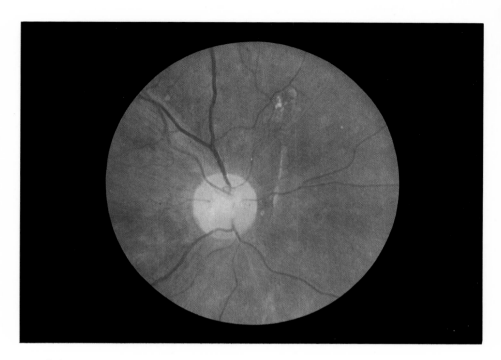

Fig. 82

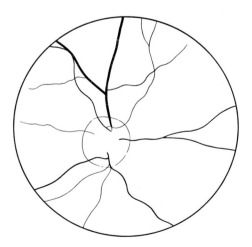

Papilloedema

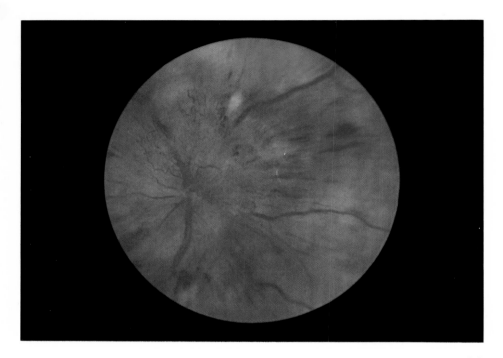

Fig. 83

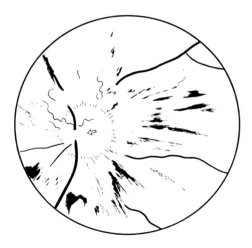

Papilloedema found in a case of pheochromocytoma.

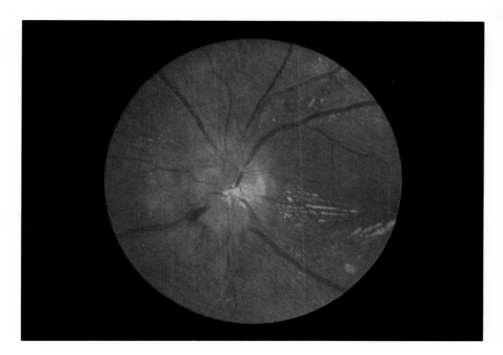

Fig. 84

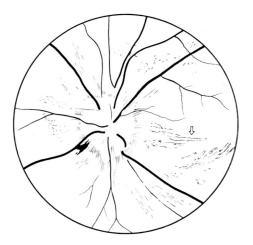

Papilloedema found in a case of
chronic glomerulonephritis.

Optic neuritis

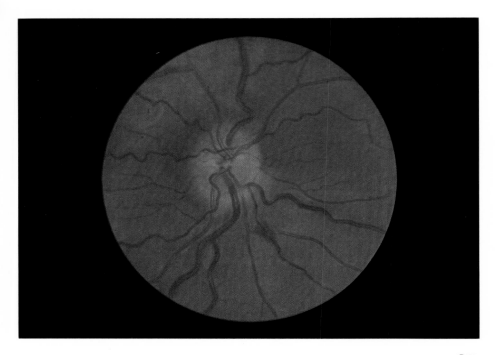

Fig. 85

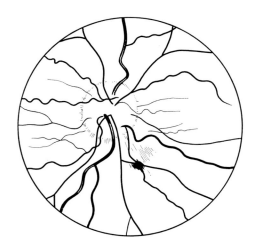

Retinal oedema

When there are circulatory disturbances in the retinal blood system, retinal oedema appears in the regions served by it. Oedema is observed as an abnormal reflex or a milky grayish opacity. In some cases of toxaemia of pregnancy or glomerulonephritis, a transparent circumscribed retinal oedema with a relatively distinct margin is observed ("glasiges Ödem").

Note (Fig. 88):

> After the disappearance of retinal oedema, punctiform hard spots sometimes appear at that place. These hard spots are called oedəma residue.

Retinal oedema

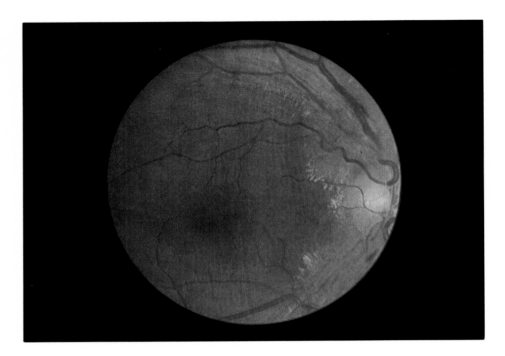

Fig. 86

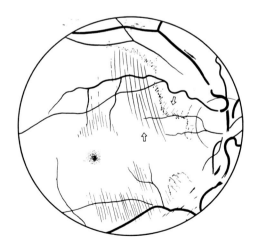

Retinal oedema (glasiges Ödem)

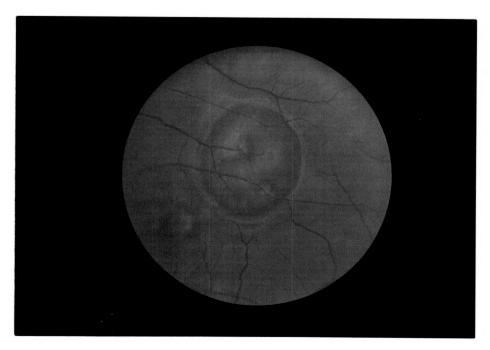

Fig. 87

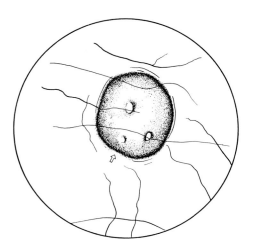

So-called oedema residue

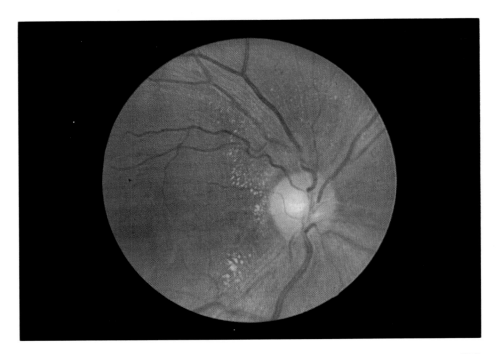

Fig. 88

Detachment of the retina
(Fig. 89, 90)

This is secondary detachment of the retina due to subretinal exudate. The detached area appears grayish white and elevated. This appears bilaterally in most cases.

Retinal detachment (of slight grade)

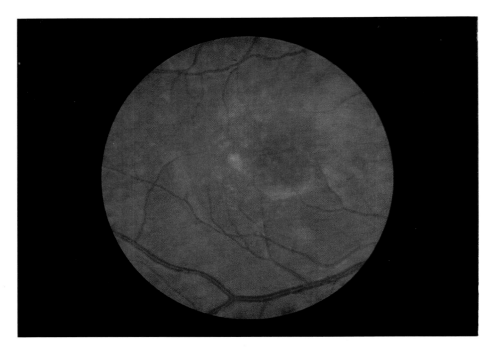

Fig. 89

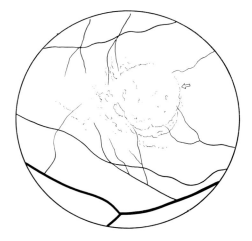

Retinal detachment (of moderate grade)

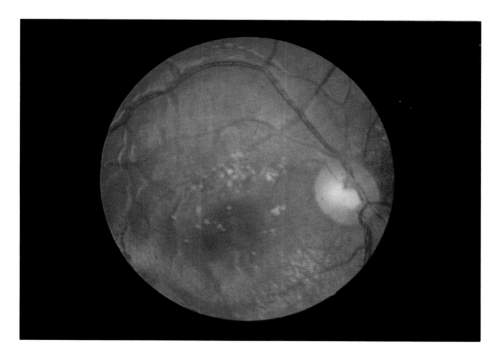

Fig. 90

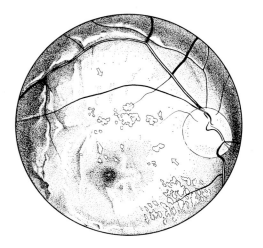

Degenerative focus (Fig. 91)

Degenerative foci with pigmented or depigmented spots are shown especially at the macular area.

Degenerative foci with pigment spots

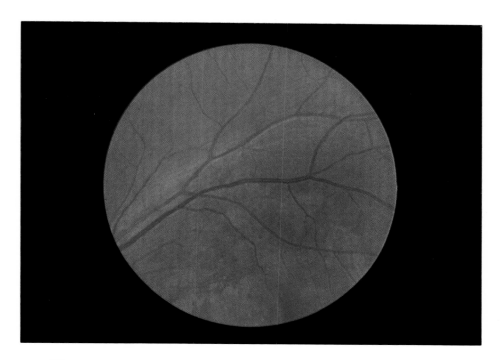

Fig. 91

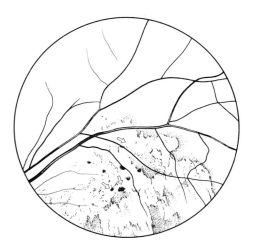

Supplementary diagnostic method

The following methods are available for differential diagnosis:

i) Measurement of the calibre of the arteriole over a period of time —for the assessment of the presence of narrowness or narrowing, and differentiation between functional narrowing and organic narrowing.

ii) Load-tests such as injection of vasodilating or vasoconstricting agents, and cold pressor test—for differential diagnosis of functional narrowing and organic narrowing.

iii) Fluorescein fundus angiography—for differentiation of apparent narrowing and real narrowing, or differentiation between spotty haemorrhage and microaneurysm.

iv) Ophthalmoscopy using red-free light—for judgment of the presence of perivascular stripe, opacification of the arteriolar wall and retinal oedema.

Classification of Fundus Changes in Hypertension

As for fundus changes in hypertensive diseases, when the change is great in degree, general conditions tend to be grave, resulting in an elevation of the mortality rate; therefore a classification relating the grade of the change and the seriousness of the disease was attempted.

THIEL's classification (1936, 1948), KEITH-WAGENER-BARKER's classification (1939) (called KEITH-WAGENER's classification, K.-W. classification), WAGENER-CLAY-GIPNER's classification (1947), SCHEIE's classification (1953) and LEISHMAN's classification (1957) are known world-wide. In Japan, KEITH-WAGENER's classification and SCHEIE's classification and some classifications modified from these two are in use.

All the above-mentioned classifications are based on principles, which are more or less different, so we have classified them in the following 3 groups:

1) Using SCHEIE's classification and its modification. We classified the changes appearing in the fundus of hypertensives into:

    (1)   Arteriolar sclerosis, which is considered as organic and almost irreversible,

    (2)   Hypertensive change, which is considered as functional and largely reversible,

and furthermore classified into four grades the extent of the fundus changes. Fundus changes due to hypertension and supposed to consist chiefly of mixtures of the above-mentioned two groups: Various changes will result in various other forms.

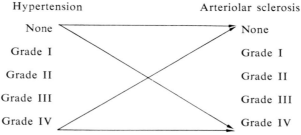

Fig. 1　Mutual relations of the grades of retinal changes of hypertension and retinal arteriolar sclerosis (SCHEIE, 1953)

This classification was very convenient for understanding fundus changes in hypertension, for educating medical researchers, and for considering separately arteriolar sclerosis and hypertensive changes.

2) Classification according to systemic diseases. In cases of essential hypertension, fundus changes are different in the benign and in the malignant group. Starting from this clinical fact, we estimate the nature of the hypertension by the all-round fundus findings and vice-versa. Representative of this method is the KEITH-WAGENER's classification. According to this classification, the fundus changes are classified into 4 groups in a sense : benign, semi-benign, semi-malignant and malignant. The THIEL's classification in Germany resembles this one, and may be called the same kind of classification. WAGENER-CLAY-GIPNER's classification is designed to classify into 5 grades the nature of the hypertension, including essential hypertension and other hypertensive conditions, judging from the nature of the fundus changes.

3) Classification centering on involutionary sclerosis of the arteriole. Representative of this classification is LEISHMAN's system. With aging, involutionary sclerosis appearing in the artery system, especially in the arteriolar system, may be one of the mechanisms defending the living body against the abnormal rise of blood pressure.

From this point of view, we consider, according to the distribution and extent of the individual involutionary sclerosis at the time of the start of hypertension, the process and nature of the hypertension thereafter becomes different, and the fundus changes may be classified into 7 groups.

We explain these classifications as follows :

A. SCHEIE's Classification (1953)

The content of SCHEIE's classification is in Table 1.

Table 1 SCHEIE's classification (1953)

Kind of change / Grade	Sclerotic changes	Hypertensive changes
Grade I	Reflex of arteriolar stripe increased, arteriovenous crossing signs of slight grade are found.	The retinal arterioles reveal a slight generalized narrowing, however no obvious calibre-irregularity. In the periphery from the 2nd branch of the retinal artery sometimes severe narrowing is found.
Grade II	Marked reflex-increase; moderate crossing signs.	Generalized narrowing in still more pronounced and localized calibre-irregularities, indicating severe spasm, are present.
Grade III	The presence of copper-wired arteries and still more marked arteriovenous crossing phenomena.	Still more extreme narrowing and irregularity of the retinal arterioles, accompanied by retinal exudates or both.
Grade IV	Silver-wired arteries. Some times appearance of white lines.	All the signs characteristic of Grade III plus papilloedema.

Modified classification In Japan, for the purpose of facilitating and clarifying the evaluation of grade of sclerotic change by SCHEIE's classification, a classification centering on arterio-venous crossing phenomena has been made.

Here, slight grade (1st grade), moderate grade (2 nd grade), and severe grade or special grade (3 rd- 4 th grade) of the arterio-venous crossing sign are respectively similar to those of the Keio-University modification (Table 2).

In addition, SCHEIE's classification as modified by the Tokyo Research Council for the Control of Cerebrocardiovascular Diseases is also used (Table 3).

On the other hand, the classification by the Tohoku University Department of Ophthalmology combines the modified method of SCHEIE's classification and KEITH-WAGENER's classification, but it is chiefly based upon SCHEIE's point of view, so it might be called a sort of modified SCHEIE's classification.

Table 2 Standard for grading of retinal arteriolar sclerosis
(Keio-University modification of SCHEIE's classification, 1957~1958)

Grade	Fundus-findings
1st grade	At the crossed area the vein, which runs under the artery, shows slight turgescence or depression in contact with that artery.
2nd grade	At the arterio-venous crossing apparently obvious changes have occurred, but no concealment and interruption is found.
3rd grade	The blood column of the vein is interrupted and concealed at the crossed part.
4th grade	Silver-wired artery reveals itself; changes of 3rd grade become very marked.

Note: 1. In this classification special importance is attached to the arteriovenous crossing phenomenon.
2. Crossing signs within 1 PD distal from the optic disc are disregarded.

Table 3 Tokyo Cerebro-Cardiovascular Research Committee modification of SCHEIE's classification (1966)

Grade	Hypertensive changes	Grade	Sclerotic changes
grade 0	Normal	grade 0	Normal
grade 1	Arteriolar narrowing (+) and/or calibre-irregularity (+)	grade 1	Arterio-venous crossing signs (+) and/or arteriolar reflex (+)
grade 2	Arteriolar narrowing (++) and/or calibre-irregularity (++)	grade 2	Arteriolar crossing (++) or copper-wired artery
grade 3	Spotty or patchy haemorrhage except thrombosis of the retinal central vein	grade 3	Arteriolar crossing and copper-wired artery, white line crossing signs (+++) or silver-wired (white lined)
grade 3 +Retino-pathies	Grade 3 +cotton-wool patches or retinal oedema	grade 4	Arterio-venous crossing sign (++) and silver-wired or white lined artery
grade 4	Grade 3+retinopathy+ papilloedema	N (not classifiable)	
others	H 0 or 1 grade+artery with haemorrhage, hard patch, soft patch on oedema		
N (not classifiable)			

124

Table 4 Tohoku-University classification

		Hypertonic changes		Sclerotic changes			
Changes of the retinal arteriole	1 st grade	Partial focal narrowing of slight grade (Tendency to straightening)		The arteriolar wall shows decrease in transparency and increased reflex (Tendency to elongation and tortuosity)		1 st grade	Changes of the retinal arteriole
	2 nd grade (vein)	Narrowing of moderate grade, calibre-irregularity (acute-angled branching) (humping, deviation)		Marked turgescence and thickening of the arteriolar wall. Arterio-venous crossing phenomenon (obtuse-angled branching) tapering, arching, concealment, nicking, banking, parallel-compression.		2 nd grade (vein)	
	3 rd grade	Severe narrowing (angiospasm)	with corkscrew-liked tortuosity of the pre-capillary and retinal changes complicated	Copper-wired artery	Severe arterio-sclerosis and complication of the retinal changes	3 rd grade	
	4 th grade	Severe narrowing (ischemia)		Silver-wired artery, white sheathing		4 th grade	
Changes of the optic disc and retina		Papilloedema, papillanaemia, opacity and oedema of the retina, exudative haemorrhage, cotton-wool-patches, hyalinous oedema, secondary retinal detachment		Obstruction of the vein (thrombosis), retinal haemorrhage, neovascularization, arteriovenous anastomosis, glial tissue proliferation, hard patches, star figure, pigment spot, occlusion of the retinal arteriole, optic atrophy, arteriosclerosis of the choroid			Changes of the optic disc and retina
Diagnosis of the fundus changes		Arteriolohypertonus retinae (I) (Fundus hypertonicus)					Diagnosis of the fundus changes
		Retinopathia hypertonica s. angiospastica (III)		Arteriolosclerosis retinae (IIa)			
		Neuroretinopathia hypertonica s. angiospastica (IV)		Retinopathia arteriolosclerotica (IIb)			
General state				Blood pressure mmHg			
Synthetic diagnosis							Examiner

B. KEITH-WAGENER's Classification (1939)

The fundus changes are classified in 4 groups.

Group 1: The fundus change is slight, and slight narrowing and sclerosis are seen in the arterioles.

Group 2: The change in the arterioles is more remarkable than that of the group 1.

Group 3: Remarkable hypertonus and spasm are recognized in the retinal arterioles, including sclerotic changes. Such changes are wide-spread and obvious, with slight or obvious angiospastic retinopathy (hypertensive retinopathy).

Group 4: Functional and organic narrowing in the retinal arterioles with wide-spread angiospastic retinopathy (hypertensive retinopathy) is seen, and there is an extensive papilloedema.

Some remarks concerning judgment.

(1) In the group 1, the functions of the retina, brain, heart and kidney are in good condition. The blood pressure is sometimes variable, or tends to rise to a certain extent, on occasion.

(2) Obstruction (thrombosis) of the retinal vein is generally regarded as group 2.

(3) Arteriosclerotic retinopathy (FOSTER MOORE) is regarded as group 2, except cases where the change is considered as based upon past angiospastic retinopathy.

(4) With clear sclerotic change of the retinal arterioles, if there is angiospastic retinopathy, it is regarded as group 3 or group 4.

(5) Functional disorders are apt to appear in the organs relating to the arterial system. In the group 4 such a disorder usually appears in marked severity, with some exceptions. Judgment is made chiefly on the basis of the respective fundus changes.

(6) Even if there are remarkable differences in calibre, suggesting angiospasm in the retinal arterial tree, it is regarded as group 2 in cases of non-hypertensive retinopathy, and the process is followed carefully.

(7) The distinctive feature of the group 3 consists of papilloedema and wide-spread angiospastic retinopathy.

(8) In cases where there is a remarkable arteriolar sclerosis preceding with papilloedema and angiospastic retinopathy, it is regarded as group 4. But, if these conditions are not fully present, placement in the group 4 should be made with great caution. Judgment should be made not only by fundus change, but also by the general condition and clinical examination of the patient.

(9) One must be careful to distinguish acute angiospastic retinopathy. The special feature of this disease is the lack of sclerotic change (organic change of the vascular wall) if there is any angiospastic finding (perivascular narrowing of the arteriole and different calibre). Sometimes we can not distinguish both.

(10) Relations between SCHEIE's classification and KEITH-WAGENER's classification. To judge by SCHEIE's classification gives us the key to KEITH-WAGENER's classification. The mutual relations are noted in Figure 2.

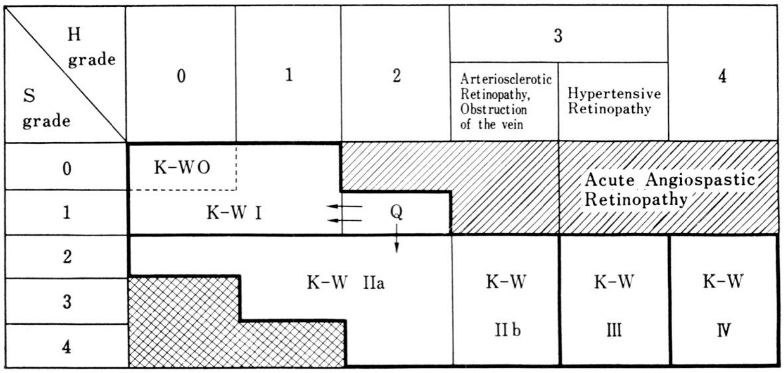

S grade \ H grade	0	1	2	3 (Arteriosclerotic Retinopathy, Obstruction of the vein)	3 (Hypertensive Retinopathy)	4
0	K-W O	K-W I	← Q		Acute Angiospastic Retinopathy	
1						
2		K-W IIa		K-W IIb	K-W III	K-W IV
3						
4						

Fig. 2 Relations between SCHEIE's classification and KEITH-WAGENER's classification (KATOH and MATSUI, 1964).

Note: 1) S: sclerotic change, H: hypertensive change
2) In cases which are distinctly diagnosed as essential hypertension, K-W O Group are little recognizable, however, if it exists, such change should be considered to be a part of K-W I Group.
3) ▨ In cases of essential hypertension rarely discerned.
▩ Such case is hardly discerned as well logically as practically.
4) A case as Q marking shows rather than otherwise the character of K-W I Group.

127

C. KEITH-WAGENER's Classification and its Modification

In Japan, the methods modified by Keio-University and the Chiba-University method have come into wide use.

Table 5 Keio-University modification of KEITH-WAGENER's classification

	Grouping by KEITH-WAGENER's classification		Fundus change
Normal fundus	Group I		(S_0H_0) none (rare) (K-W 0 group)
			Slight narrowing and sclerosis of the retinal arteriole (SCHEIE's modification grade I)
Fundus hypertonicus	Group II	a	Arteriolar sclerosis becomes marked (SCHEIE's grade II), and narrowing is more marked than Group I
		b	Arteriosclerotic retinopathy or obstruction of the retinal central vein is added to the above-mentioned
Retinopathia hypertonica	Group III		An important criterion is the presence of angio-spastic retinitis, together with definite sclerotic changes in the arterioles, namely retinal oedema, white spot, haemorrhage
	Group IV		The important retinal alterations are marked spastic and organic narrowing of the arterioles, with diffuse retinitis and oedema of the discs

The important points of the Keio-University modification are mentioned below :

(1) When judgment is made according to the group, the grade of arteriolar sclerosis must be made according to SCHEIE's classification or by the Keio-modified method.

(2) In order to be included in the group II, the grade of arteriolar sclerosis must be over grade II (moderate grade) by SCHEIE's classification.

(3) The group II is divided into IIa and IIb. Cases of non-bleeding and white patches on the retina are IIa. Cases of bleeding and white patch on the retina are IIb. Therefore most cases of arteriosclerotic retinopathy, obstruction of the vein (branch), are judged as group IIb.

The important points of the Chiba-University-modified method are mentioned below :

(1) The group II is divided into IIa, IIb and IIc. Group IIa is for the moderate grade of arteriolar sclerosis. Group IIb is for high grade and Group IIc is similar to Group IIb of Keio-University-modified K-W classification.

(2) The group III is divided into IIIa and IIIb.

Group IIIa applies when retinal oedema is limited and IIIb applies when retinal oedema is extensive.

D. WAGENER-CLAY-GIPNER's Classification (1947)

Hypertension, including essential hypertension and other hypertensive diseases, is divided into 5 groups, according to its nature at the time of examination. Placement into each group is possible on the basis of fundus changes. This classification is very much like KEITH-WAGENER's classification, except in the notes on the fundus findings of acute hypertension.

Table 6 WAGENER-CLAY-GIPNER's classification (1947)

	Characteristics of fundus changes
Neurogenic hypertension	No changes except slight diffuse narrowing are found, even in cases of long-standing elevation of the blood pressure
Acute (angiospastic) hypertension	In this case the arterioles show generalized narrowing and localized narrowness, usually accompanied by retinal oedema, cotton-wool patch, haemorrhage, and sometimes papilloedema.
Chronic non-progressive (benign) hypertension	At the early stage, generalized narrowing of the arteriole is recognized. In cases where hypertension has continued for several years, a slight diffuse arteriolosclerosis appears.
Chronic progressive hypertension	Usually, generalized arteriosclerotic changes, and further localized constriction, and often circumscribed sclerosis are found. However, cotton-wool patches and haemorrhage are found.
Terminal malignant hypertension	Usually, there is diffuse arteriolosclerosis and papilloedema, besides generalized arteriolar narrowing, focalized constriction, focalized narrowing, retinal haemorrhage, retinal oedema, and cotton-wool patches. Oedema residue (hard spots) and macular star-figure are found.

E. LEISHMAN's Classification (1957)

The fundus changes in hypertension are divided into the following 7 groups.

1) Involutionary sclerosis (fundus finding)
2) Involutionary sclerosis with hypertension (fundus finding)
3) Advanced involutionary sclerosis with hypertension (fundus finding)
4) The normal fundus in youth, with normal blood pressure readings
5) Early hypertension in youthful vessels
6) Fulminating hypertension
7) Severe hypertension with reactive sclerosis

Table 7 LEISHMAN's classification (1957)
(Clinical classification of fundus pictures in hypertension and arteriosclerosis)

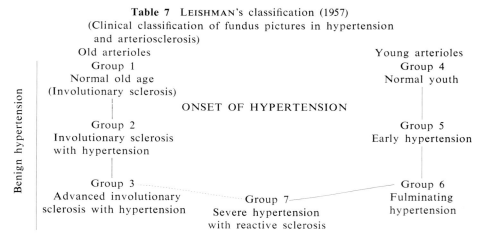

Table 8 Characteristics of the groups of LEISHMAN's classification

Group	General conditions	Ophthalmoscopic findings
1 Involutionary sclerosis	Universal after 60 years. Usually systolic blood pressure elevated, but diastolic not so elevated.	Reflexes are diminished, the hue is dull, retinal pigmentation is disturbed. Retinal arteries run a relatively straight course, are diffusely narrow and slightly pale, and tend to branch at an acute angle. The walls are not visible.
2 Involutionary sclerosis with hypertension	Blood pressure 200/95~120. This type seems to represent hypertension occurring in arterioles already partially defended by patchy sclerosis. Primary sclerosis predetermines the benign course of hypertensive disorder.	Large arterioles remain straight and narrow, but small arterioles becomes more red, wide and curvilinear. There is no concealment of the vein at arteriovenous crossings. The veins distal to some of the crossings show more intense colour and congestion.

Table 8 (continued)

Group	General conditions	Ophthalmoscopic findings
3 Advanced involutionary sclerosis with hypertension	Blood pressure levels of a higher order than in group 2. The patient may have no complaints, and may be unaware of hypertension, though diastolic pressure may reach 140 mmHg.	The main retinal arterioles are red, wide, and tortuous. Peripheral arterioles are relatively pale, straight, and narrow. There is no concealment of the vein at arteriovenous crossings, but congestion of the vein is present distal to some of these crossings.
4 The normal fundus in youth		The optic disc has a healthy pink colour, the retinal arterioles are wide, well-coloured, and sinuous. The reflexes are bright and rich in hue. The fundus background had a glittering quality and the retinal pigmentation is uniform.
5 Early hypertension in youthful vessels	This type represents diffuse hypertonus, the initial response of youthful vessels in the hypertensive state. Transient hypertension is often associated with acute glomerulonephritis or toxaemia of pregnancy.	When high blood pressure is present, it can be distinguished by diffuse constriction of the retinal arterioles, which appear straight and narrow, with a blood column of diminished colour intensity. There is no concealment of the veins at arterio-venous crossings, but congestion of the vein is present distal to some crossings.
6 Fulminating hypertension	This type is usually called "malignant" hypertension; the term "fulminating" is to be preferred. It need not be construed as a separate type of hypertension, but rather as an acutely progressive disorder resulting from a very severe hypertensive stimulus acting upon relatively youthful arterioles which are undefended by fibrosis. Blood pressure 250/150 mmHg.	The papilloedema is always well marked and is often associated with oedema of the retina. The arteries remain excessively pale, diffusely narrow and become tortuous, suggesting elongation. Small vessels may be straight and narrow, suggesting hypertonus. Hard spots are usually numerous around the disc. Superficial patches of "cotton-wool" lie here and there in close relation to a small arteriole. Sometimes a thrombotic blood column is seen.
7 Severe hypertension with reactive sclerosis	This group appears to represent a severe hypertensive stimulus resulting in reactive changes; the reaction is progressing by way of hypertonus and hyperplasia into replacement fibrosis and sclerosis.	The disc is normal, or has a white haze which does not obscure the vessels in its surface. The arterioles are more tortuous than normal, and there is impediment to venous outflow at arterio-venous crossings.

IV

An Overall View

The authors have noted each method of observation and the model for description, pointing out the criteria for describing the fundus changes of hypertensive diseases.

We should measure the importance in diagnostic value of these individual fundus changes by coding or other polydimensional techniques and reexamine critically whether the meaning of the fundus changes achieve the expected purpose or not.

If we choose a good match to the grades of fundus change in hypertensive disease, it is possible to classify, them in outline as follows.

Out of all the various vascular lesions, we shall designate as "hypertonus" the fundus change of which the cardinal symptom is hypertonic ("hypertensive"); as "arteriolosclerosis" the fundus change of which the principal symptom is sclerotic, and respectively grade the degree as slight, moderate or severe. Further, we shall divide the hypertensive retinopathies as follows, according to ocular manifestations.

(1) Hypertonus of the retinal arteriole
    slight grade   (I)
    moderate grade   (II)
    severe grade   (III)
(2) Retinal arteriolosclerosis
    slight grade   (I)
    moderate grade   (II)
    severe grade   (III)
(3) Hypertensive retinopathy
    a) arteriosclerotic retinopathy
    b) angiospastic retinopathy
    c) angiospastic neuroretinopathy

Because this classification is a diagnosis based upon symptoms, in accordance with the origin of the disease, the type may be a mixture of more than two names.

For example in nephrosclerosis, hypertonus is concurrent with retinal arteriolosclerosis.

When the initial letters of the finding is written in addition to its grade in ophthalmological use, this is very convenient and available for investigation of the alteration of lesions and the progress and course of the basic disease.

Moreover we must contribute to the diagnosis of the original diseases by distinct observations of fundus and synthetic consideration of lesions in various other organs.

Hypertonus of the retinal arteriole

In general, when tonus (slight continuous contraction of a muscle) occurs in the wall of a retinal arteriole, that same portion is narrowed so the blood column appears to be thin and straightened, accompanied with a somewhat whitish reflex. Moreover, if such tonus is focal, the retinal arteriole upstream from the corresponding part often shows compensatory elevation of the blood pressure following increase of the cardiac output, dilatation of the blood column, active pulsatile phenomenon, and other transient hypertonic conditions.

Especially in the case of circumscribed hypertonus in a terminal arteriole distal from the second branch which has by nature a physiologically thin blood column, the finding of a narrowed blood column is often passed over; rather the sight of dilatation in the upper stream grasps the observer's attention.

However, if there is active hypertonus of the arteriole at the thicker part, one can, with some attention, easily find narrowing of the retinal arteriole and distinguish active (automatic) hypertonus from passive hypertonus. More frequently there are phenomena of calibre-irregularity. As mentioned above, fundus views where hypertonic condition is a cardinal symptom are called hypertonus of the retinal arteriole. Also, a few sclerotic changes such as arterio-venous crossing signs may be found, too.

These fundus changes are seen very frequently in patients with hypertensive disease in an early stage.

Retinal arteriolosclerosis

The wall of a blood vessel begins to show tissue proliferation in a tendency to increase its thickeness and length as a compensatory change when hypertonus continues in the wall of the arteriole over a long period of time, or if a specific metabolic disturbance lasts for some time. This is so-called retinal arteriolosclerosis. The vascular changes in each organ are neither always uniform or similar, and differ somewhat in velocity and severity besides.

In the retina, the walls of the artery or arteriole thicken and decrease in transparency. Ophthalmoscopically, opacity or reflex-increase of the vessel-wall is seen. When the observer is unable to distinguish between increase of reflex stripe and widening of reflex stripe due to increased tension, he may induce an ischemic condition by putting pressure on the eyeball; as a result the former will remain while the latter will disappear (Salus' explanation).

As such thickening of the vessel wall increases, arterio-venous crossing sign, copper-wired artery, silver-wired artery, sheathing and other findings appear.

Concomitantly with these changes, the length of the arteriole increases and sometimes shows less tortuosity.

The fundus picture, which has the above-mentioned arteriosclerotic changes as the main constituents, is retinal arteriolosclerosis.

In atheromatous arteriosclerosis, a spotty plaque at the thickened portion of the arteriole that circumscribes only a part of the vessel wall may very rarely be seen.

After all, this is the fundus picture to which importance is attached by the internist, because it denotes the existence of similar organic changes in the arterioles of the brain and kidneys especially.

Arteriosclerotic retinopathy

Arteriosclerotic changes reach not only the arteries but also the arterioles and at same time cause in the retinal arterioles decreased elasticity, narrowing of the vascular lumen, and increase in resistance of the blood stream, obstruction of the lumen deeper in the proper layer of the retina, haemorrhage, venous obstruction (thrombosis), compensatory neovascularization, anastomosis of the retinal vessels, proliferated tissue, white patches, pigment spots, atrophied foci, and other changes.

These fundus pictures, which are named arteriosclerotic retinopathy, appear also in cases where angiospastic changes are interrupted following adequate treatment.

Angiospastic retinopathy

When a hypertonic state in the arteriole occurs violently or abruptly accompanied by abnormal excitation of its wall, it appears clearly in the form of angiospasm, followed, not always sufficiently by a compensatory mechanism.

In such a case various changes may spring up in the proper layer of the retina besides. There are various hypotheses concerning the mechanism of the appearance of the retinal changes.

The first is the so-called peristatic or ischemic theory, that such retinal change occurs chiefly at the peripheral area with rather low arterial pressure (by ELWYN). In the retinal arteriolar system marked spastic contraction with calibre-irregularity appears, and the downstream falls into a paretic state because of ischemia. Therefore peristasis of the bloodstream, changes of the wall-permeability, inverse dilatation, stasis and corkscrew-like tortuosity are seen, while sclerotic changes are relatively few.

The second is an opposite opinion. It is the hypertensive or plethoric theory by SCHROEDER, that the retinal changes appear rather at an area with high diastolic pressure. For instance, haemorrhage and exudation of the retina are involved when compensatory insufficiency of the blood vessel-wall correspond to abnormal elevation of the diastolic pressure, because arteriolar spasm brings on transitive hypertonus upstream.

Next is the toxic or intoxication theory (by KOYANAGI). According to this opinion the pathologic changes of the retinal vascular endothelium and the retinal pigment epithelium have a respective resemblance to that of the blood vessels in the kidney and brain and the ureteral epithelium of the kidney and choroidal plexus epithelium of the cranial ventricle, because it is out of the bounds of possibility that the mechanism of these retinal changes can be explained as a simple mechanical lesion of circular disturbance.

However that may be, the picture that is named as nephritic retinopathy, is included in this category. The fundus change occurs initially in the papillomacular field, from which a capillary net develops and has a characteristic appearance.

The change found in toxaemia of pregnancy is similar. Some maladies, which are of endocrine origin, reveal the same symptoms.

Angiospastic neuroretinopathy

Acute, severe types of the above-mentioned angiospastic retinopathy, that have particular fundus pictures with marked neuroretinal oedema or papilloedema are specifically designated as angiospastic neuroretinopathy.

These types are accompanied by hyaline oedema, subretinal fluid and secondary retinal detachment occuring, simultaneously with an elevation of the intracranial pressure. In pheochromocytoma, angiospastic neuroretinopathy occurs in typical acute cases.

REFERENCES

1) ARAI, H. and NAKAJIMA, A.: Elapsed Observation on Fundus Changes of Hypertensive (XXII Group-Discussion on Hypertensive Retinopathy) Jap. J. Clin. Ophthalm. 23, 1231, 1969.

2) CHIGUSA, M.: Studies on the Branching-off Angles of the Precapillary Arteries from the Retinal Artery with Special Reference to the Effect of Systemic Hypertension upon the Angles. Acta. Soc. Ophthalm. Jap. 68, 575, 1964.

3) ELWYN, H.: Diseases of the Retina. Blakiston, London, 1947.

4) FOSTER MOORE, R.: The Retinal Circulation in Arterio-Sclerosis. Trans. Ophthalm. Soc. Unit. King., 36, 329, 1916.

5) FOSTER MOORE, R.: The Retinitis of Arteriosclerosis and its Relation to Retinitis and to Cerebral Vascular Disease. Brit. J. Ophthalm. 1, 372, 1917.

6) HARA, K.: Criteria and its description of the Fundus Changes in Hypertension. Folia Ophthalm. Jap. 2, 63, 1958.

7) HARA, K.: Criteria of Fundus Changes in Gothenburg Meeting (WHO). Ophthalmology (Japanese) 7, 308, 1965.

8) HARA, K. et al.: Standard for grading of Arteriovenous Crossing Phenomenon (XXI Group-discussion on Hypertensive Retinopathy) Jap. J. Clin. Ophthalm. 22, 1221, 1968.

9) HAYAKAWA, H.: Studies on the Measurement of Retinal Blood Vessels. Report I. Especially on the Curve Ratio of Retinal Blood Vessels. Acta Soc. Ophthalm. Jap. 71, 509, 1967.

10) HAYAKAWA, H.: Studies on the Measurement of Retinal Blood Vessels. Report II. Curve Ratio and Course Ratio of the Retinal Blood Vessels on the Disease Accompanied by Hypertension. Acta Soc. Ophthalm. Jap. 71, 1607, 1967.

11) HAYAKAWA, H.: Studies on the Measurement of Retinal Blood Vessels. Report III. The Curve Ratio of fine Venous Branches at the Macula Lutea on Hypertensive Fundus. Report IV. The Curve Ratio and Course Ratio of Retinal Blood Vessels in the Cases of Diseases of Blood Vessel System and Diseases Related to them. Acta Soc. Ophthalm. Jap. 72, 1315, 1968.

12) HISATOMI, C.: Studies on the Retinal Vascular Calibre by Means of Fundus Photomicrometry. Rep. I. Fluctuation of Calibres. Acta Soc. Ophthalm. Jap. 46, 2582, 1960.

13) HOLLENHORST, R. W.: Significance of Bright Plaques in the Retinal Arterioles. J. A. M. A. 178, 23, 1961.

14) IKUI, H.: Discussion to Reference 10). Acta Soc. Ophthalm. Jap. 71, 1636~1637, 1966.

15) IRINODA, K.: Fundus Change and its References to General Pathological Findings in Hypertension. (Japanese) Jap. Medical J. 2308, 10, 1968.

16) ISHIKAWA, K.: Essential Hypertension and its Fundus Changes. (Report I) Jap. Rev. Clin. Ophthalm. 52, 618, 1958.

17) KATOH, K.: A Trial to standardize the Japanese Ophthalmological Termi-
nology of Hypertensive Fundus Changes by the Members of Researching
Group of Hypertension. Acta Soc. Ophthalm. Jap. 69, 2086, 1965.

18) KATOH, K. et al.: Some Findings in the Fundus in Relation with Blood
Pressure (No. 1) Classification of Hypertensive Changes of the Fundus
and its Results. Jap. J. Clin. Ophthalm. 11, 1017, 1957.

19) KATOH, K. and MATSUI, M.: Hypertension, Diabetes Mellitus and its
Fundus Changes (Japanese). II Edition, Kanehara & Co., Tokyo, 1966.

20) KEITH, N. M., WAGENER, H. P. and BARKER, M. W.: Some Different
Types of Essential Hypertension. Trans. Amer. Ophthalm. Soc. 45, 57,
1947.

21) KINUKAWA, K.: Studies on Changes of the Retinal Arterioles in Hypertension. Report II. On the Curve Ratio of the Retinal Blood Vessel.
Acta Soc. Ophthalm. Jap. 69, 2058, 1965.

22) KIRISAWA, N. and KUWAJIMA, J.: Ophthalmoscopic Observation on Hypertension. 92, (Japanese) Nankodo, Tokyo, 1964.

23) KOYANAGI, Y.: Veränderungen an der Netzhaut bei Hochdruck. Patho-
logische Anatomie. Acta XV Concilium Ophthalmologicum (Cairo) 1,
143, 1938.

24) KUNITOMO, N. et al.: Studies on the Hypertension from the Photograph
of the Fundus I. Variation of the Diameter of Retinal Blood Vessels
on Cold Pressure Test. Acta Soc. Ophthalm. Jap. 68, 827, 1964.

25) KUNITOMO, N. et al.: Narrowing and Spasmus of Retinal Small Arteries.
Acta Soc. Ophthalm. Jap. 70, 1240, 1966.

26) KUWAJIMA, J.: Pictures of Ocular Fundus in Diffuse Arteriolar Diseases
with Hypertension. Jap. J. Clin. Ophthalm. 13, 589, 1959.

27) LEISHMAN, R.: The Eye in General Vascular Disease Hypertension and
Arteriosclerosis. Brit. J. Ophthalm. 41, 641, 1957.

28) MATSUBAYASHI, M. et al.: Studies on the Rate of Calibres of Central
Retinal Artery and Vein on the Photograph of the Fundus. Acta Soc.
Ophthalm. Jap. 64, 1949, 1960.

29) MATSUYAMA, S.: Photographic Micrometry of the Calibre of the Retinal
Arteries and the Width of the Reflex Streaks (Report I). Jap. J. Clin.
Ophthalm. 16, 221, 1962.

30) NAKAJIMA, A.: Ocular Fundus in Hypertension Criteria for Classification
by Fundus Colour Photographs. Tokyo Council for Control of Cerebro-
cardiovascular Diseases, 1966.

31) NAKAJIMA, A. and ARAI, H.: Abnormality of Branching Angle of the
Retinal Arteriole (XXI Group-Discussion on Hypertensive Retinopathy)
Jap. J. Clin. Ophthalm. 22, 1220, 1968.

32) NORDENSON, C.: Farbenaufnahmen des toten Augenhintergrundes (Deu-
tsch. Ophth. Ges. Heidelberg, 1928). cit. Zbl. f. Ophth. 20, 209, 1929.
Ibid: Stereoskopische Kammer für Aufnahmen des Augenhintergrundes
(XIII Internationaler Ophthalmologenkongress, Amsterdam, Den Haag,
Scheveningen 1929). cit. Zbl. f. Ophth. 22,738, 1930.

33) PILLAT, A.: Some Remarks on Changes of the Eye Ground in Toxaemia
in Pregnancy. Chinese Med. J. XLVI: 149, 1932.

34) SALUS, R.: A Contribution to the Diagnosis of Arteriosclerosis and
Diagnosis of Arteriosclerosis and Hypertension. Am. J. Ophthalm. 45,
Part 1, 81, 1958.

35) SCHEIE, H. G. : Evaluation of Ophthalmoscopic Changes of Hypertension and Arteriolar Sclerosis. AMA Arch. Ophthalm. 49, 117, 1953.

36) SCHROEDER, H. A. : Mechanisms of Hypertension with a Consideration of Atherosclerosis. Thomas Springfield, Illinois, 1957.

37) SEITZ, R. : Über die scheinbare und wirkliche Änderung der Blutsäulebreite der Netzhautgefässe. Klin. Mbl. Augenhlk., 149, 1, 1966.

38) SHELBURNE, S. A. : Hypertensive Retinal Disease, 28, Grune & Stratton, New York, 1965.

39) STOKOE, N. L. and TURNER, R. W. D. : Normal Retinal Vascular Pattern. Arteriovenous Ratio as a Measure of Arterial Calibre. Brit. J. Ophthalm. 50, 21, 1966.

40) SUZUKI, T. : Measurements of the Calibre of Retinal Blood Vessels and the Width of Light Streaks in the Patients with Arteriosclerotic Hypertension. Acta Soc. Ophthalm. Jap. 65, 2164, 1961.

41) TAKAHASHI, S. and MATSUYAMA, S. : On Narrowing of Retinal Arteriole in Hypertensive Diseases. Acta Soc. Opthalm. Jap. 71, 1615, 1967.

42) THIEL, R. : Bedeutung der Hochdruck und Nierenkrankheiten. Klin. Wochenschrift, 15, 126, 1936.
Ibid : Atlas der Augenkrankheiten. Georg Thieme, Stuttgart, 1948.

43) TOSAKA, K. : On the Light Streaks of the Retinal Blood Vessels in the Patients with Essential Hypertension, studied by Means of Measurement of the Width. Acta Soc. Ophthalm. Jap. 60, 772, 1956.

44) UEMURA, M. and KATOH, K. : Retinal Diseases Accompanied by Elevation of Blood Pressure. Nichigan Zensho Vol. 22 (II) 217~587, Kanehara & Co., Tokyo, 1960.

45) WAGENER, H. P. and KEITH, N. M. : Diffuse Arteriolar Disease with Hypertension and the Associated Retinal Lesions. Medicine, 18, 317, 1939.

INDEX

139

impending obstruction of the central
    retinal vein 85
increase in reflex of the arteriolar wall
                                        25
— — tortuosity 40
— — — of the arterioles 41, 43, 44
— — — — — venules 41, 45, 46
— of the arteriolar reflex 30, 31
— arteriolar reflex 29, 32
indentation 5
— narrowness 5
inverse crossing phenomenon 50
involutionary sclerosis 130
irregular narrowness 5
— reflex-increase 26

K

Kapillarenzeichnung, vermehrte 41
Keio-University modification of KEITH-
    WAGENER's classification 128
— — — — SCHEIE's classification 123, 124
KEITH-WAGENER's classification
                            121, 126, 128
— —, Chiba-University modification
                                    128
— —, Keio-University modification 128
— —, modification 128
KEITH-WAGENER-BARKER's classification
                                    121

L

LEISHMAN's classification 121, 130
load-test 120
localized narrowness 2, 5
— (circumscribed) narrowness 2
— reflex-increase 26

M

measurement of the calibre of the art-
    eriole over a period of time 120
medullated nerve fibre 83
mixed type of arteriolar narrowing
                                    6, 22
— — — — narrowness 6
myopic eye, fundus of a 23

N

narrowing 5
—, angiospastic 3, 6, 18, 19
—, arteriolar 6
—, functional 6, 20
—, hypertonic 6
—, localized 14
—, segmental 15

narrowness 5
—, apparent 2
—, arteriolar 6, 9
—, arteriolosclerotic 6
—, diffuse 2, 5
—, focal 5
—, functional 3
—, generalized 2, 5
—, indentation 5
—, irregular 5
—, localized 2, 5
—, — (circumscribed) 2
—, organic 3, 6, 16, 17
—, partial 2
—, segmental 5
—, segmentary 5
— of retinal arterioles 2
neovascularization in the retina 92~94
— — — vitreous 96, 97
—, retinal 95
—, vitreal 95
nephritic retinopathy 135
neurogenic hypertension 129
nicking of the vein 50
normal fundus 8
— arteriolar reflex stripe 27

O

obstruction of a branch of the retinal
    vein 84
— — the central retinal vein
                            80, 84, 86~88
obtuse-angling 4
oedema residue 111, 114
opacification of the arteriolar wall 25
ophthalmoscopy using red-free light
                                    120
optic atrophy 104, 106, 107
— disc, changes of the 104
— —, pallor of the 105
— neuritis 110
organic narrowness 3, 6, 16, 17

P

pallor of the disc 104
— — — optic disc 105
papilloedema 104, 108
PARALLEL-GUNN's sign 51
partial narrowness 2
peristatic hyperaemia 41
perivascular stripe 37~39
pheochromocytoma 135
pigment spots 118
pigmentary degeneration of the retina
                                    24
post-partum 21

preretinal haemorrhage 67, 72
proliferated tissues 101~103

R

reflex from the arteriolar wall 25
— of retinal arterioles 3
— streak 25
reflex-increase, focal 26
—, irregular 26
—, localized 26
—, segmental 26
—, segmentary 26
—, of the retinal arteriole 28
retinal arteriolosclerosis 132, 133
— detachment 116, 117
— exudate 2
— haemorrhage 67~70
— neovascularization 95
retinal oedema 111~113
right-angled crossing 50

S

Salus' crossing arc 51
SCHEIE's classification 121, 123
— —, Keio-University modification
                    123, 124
— —, Tohoku-University modification
                    123, 125
— —, Tokyo Cerebro-Cardiovascular
    Research Committee modification
                    123, 124
segmental narrowing 15
— narrowness 5
— reflex-increase 26
segmentary narrowness 5
— reflex-increase 26
severe hypertension 130
sheathing of the arteriole 34~36
— — — vessels 33

soft exudate 74
— spots 74
— white spots 78, 79
spasm 3
spots, hard 74
—, — white 74~76
—, soft 74
—, — white 78, 79
star-figures 74, 77
straightening 40
— of the arterioles 41, 42

T

tapering of the vein 50
terminal malignant hypertension 129
THIEL's classification 121
Tohoku-University modification of
    SCHEIE's classification 123, 125
Tokyo Cerebro-Cardiovascular Research
    Committee modification of SCHEIE's
    classification 123, 124
tortuosity 3, 40
toxaemia, eclamptic 20

V

vein papillar ratio 3
venous obstruction 84
vermehrte Kapillarenzeichnung 41
vitreal neovascularization 95
vitreous haemorrhage 67, 73

W

WAGENER-CLAY-GIPNER's classification
                    121, 129
white patches 74
— —, circinated 81
— — found 80
white spot in the retina 74

Once Upon a Nursery Rhyme
Table of Contents

Once Upon a Nursery Rhyme

Timeless tales with rhyme, repetition, colorful characters, and simple story lines make nursery rhymes a childhood favorite. But don't let their simplicity fool you—nursery rhymes have proven to be a valuable teaching tool for young children. Not only are they a natural part of literacy learning—strengthening print awareness, phonological awareness, phonics, word study, and comprehension—but these structured stories can also open up a world of other learning!

About This Book

Once Upon a Nursery Rhyme features ten favorite rhymes and a blend of developmentally appropriate cross-curricular activities. As playful and fun as the rhymes themselves, these activities engage students in cooking, craft making, singing, playing games, and more, while promoting learning in the core curriculum areas of language arts, math, science, and social studies. You can feel confident that not only are your students delighting in the rhymes, but they are practicing essential standards-based skills!

Included in Every Unit
- A full-color rhyme mini poster suitable for lamination and sharing at circle time or posting at a circle area or center
- A reproducible mini poster appropriate for students to color and keep
- Eight cross-curricular activities labeled with age-appropriate skills
- Three or more full-color patterns suitable for laminating and using for flannelboard manipulatives, puppets, or bulletin boards or other displays
- Handy reproducible patterns to use as clip art for manipulatives, puppets, notes home, labels, or displays
- One or more reproducible pages to accompany activities or reinforce age-appropriate skills

Before Using Each Unit
- Remove the color mini poster and color patterns.
- Photocopy the back of each page.
- Cut out the patterns. Laminate the poster and patterns.
- If desired, prepare the patterns for puppet or flannelboard use.
- Store all the materials in a large, resealable plastic bag.

Managing Editor: Allison Ward
Editor at Large: Diane Badden
Staff Editors: Kim Brugger, Cindy Daoust, Leanne Stratton
Contributing Writers: Randi Austin, Valerie Corbeille, Ada Goren, Lucia Kemp-Henry, Dawn Rolita
Copy Editors: Tazmen Carlisle, Amy Kirtley-Hill, Karen L. Mayworth, Kristy Parton, Debbie Shoffner, Cathy Edwards Simrell
Cover Artist: Clevell Harris
Art Coordinator: Clint Moore
Artists: Pam Crane, Theresa Lewis Goode, Clevell Harris, Ivy L. Koonce, Clint Moore, Greg D. Rieves, Rebecca Saunders, Barry Slate, Donna K. Teal
The Mailbox® Books.com: Jennifer Tipton Bennett (DESIGNER/ARTIST); Stuart Smith (PRODUCTION ARTIST); Karen White (INTERNET COORDINATOR); Paul Fleetwood, Xiaoyun Wu (SYSTEMS)

Little Miss Muffet

Little Miss Muffet

Sat on a tuffet,

Eating her curds and whey.

There came a big spider,

Who sat down beside her

And frightened Miss Muffet away.

Little Miss Muffet

Little Miss Muffet

Sat on a tuffet,

Eating her curds and whey.

There came a big spider,

Who sat down beside her

And frightened Miss Muffet away.

Little Miss Muffet

From tuffets and spiders to curds and whey—Miss Muffet's rhyme has something for everyone! There are plenty of new words and concepts for your little learners to absorb, so pull up a tuffet and get ready for some nursery rhyme fun!

There Came a Spider
Building on prior knowledge

Create suspense among your youngsters before introducing "Little Miss Muffet" by cueing up some conversation and a quick spider survey. Hold a class discussion to reveal what your little ones already know about spiders. If necessary, add that these interesting creatures have eight legs and eat insects. Next, use this simple chart activity to find out who in your group likes spiders. Program a sheet of chart paper as shown; then put it on a table and invite each child to answer the question by writing her name (or placing her name card) in the appropriate column. With student help, count the names in each column and decide whether spiders are popular creatures.

To wrap up the activity, tell youngsters that Miss Muffet is frightened by a spider; then share the nursery rhyme on page 5.

Do You Like Spiders?	
yes	no
Abby	Micah
Remayjah	Sherman
AJ	Jason
Kelli	Bob
Mike	Claire
	Mitzi

A "Mmm-arvelous" Portrait of Miss Muffet
Identifying the beginning sound /m/

M is for *M*iss *M*uffet—and for *m*aps, *m*uffins, and *m*ayonnaise too! Your students will eagerly share /m/ words in exchange for a portrait of Miss Muffet. Have students name words with a beginning /m/ sound. As each /m/ word is named, draw a feature of Miss Muffet, beginning with a circle for her face. See how elaborate you and your class can make the portrait in five minutes!

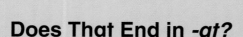
Mitten...I hear /t/ in the middle.

Sit on a Tuffet

Identifying phoneme placement

Invite your youngsters to make like Miss Muffet and sit on a tuffet for this activity! To begin, gather a small group around a special seat you designate as the tuffet. Ask students to listen as you say a word from the rhyme that contains a /t/ sound, such as *sat.* Ask whether anyone heard the /t/ sound. Where did they hear it? Was it at the beginning, in the middle, or at the end? Use *Muffet* or *little* to provide additional practice with this skill. Next, have a child stand in front of the special tuffet seat. Ask her to listen as you say a group of words and to sit on the tuffet when she hears a word with the /t/ sound. When she sits down, have her repeat the word and tell you where she heard the /t/. Repeat the activity until each child has had a turn to listen and sit on the tuffet. Terrific!

Does That End in *-at?*

*Recognizing the -*at *rime*

Review the rhyme and point out the word *sat* to your students. Write the word on your board. Then erase the *s* and write an *m* in its place. Ask whether anyone can read the word you've made. Continue substituting beginning consonants and asking for readers. Point out that each word has the same *-at* ending. Then give each child a copy of page 14. Explain that the clever spider has caught some words in its web, but it has only caught words ending with the *-at* rime. Instruct each child to cut out the words at the bottom of the page and glue only those words ending in *-at* onto the spider's web. Discuss the results as a class. Wow—that spider caught a lot of *-at* words!

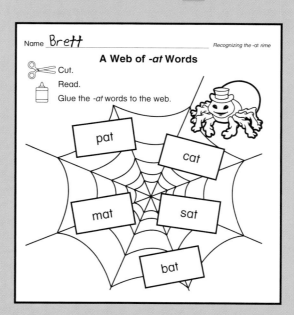

Name Brett

Recognizing the -at rime

A Web of -at Words

✂ Cut.

📖 Read.

🧴 Glue the *-at* words to the web.

pat

cat

mat

sat

bat

Eating Her...Alphabet Soup?
Blending phonemes into words

Ask a small group of students to imagine that Miss Muffet isn't eating curds and whey after all, but alphabet soup instead! Draw a large spoon outline on a magnetic board. Use magnetic letters to spell a simple consonant-vowel-consonant (CVC) word from the rhyme, such as *sat* or *big.* As you place each letter on the spoon, say its sound. Then run your finger below the finished word as you blend the sounds together. Remove the letters and spell the word a second time, this time asking students to help you say the sounds and blend them into the word. Repeat this process with another word, asking a volunteer to blend the sounds for the group to hear. Using the word bank as a guide, continue with additional CVC words until everyone has had a turn to blend a word.

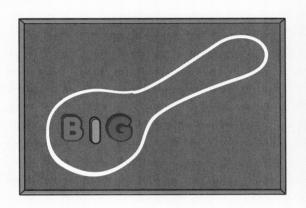

Word Bank
cat dog mat pig get hot pot peg sat net bag bug

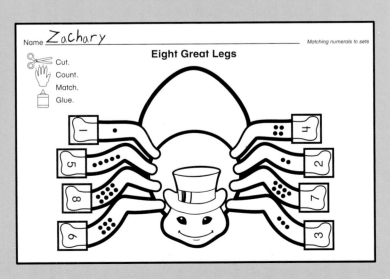

Name Zachary

Matching numerals to sets

Eight Great Legs

✂ Cut.
✋ Count.
Match.
🍼 Glue.

Eight Great Legs
Matching numerals to sets

Why was Miss Muffet scared off her tuffet when the spider came along? Perhaps its eight spindly legs frightened her! The many legs of the spider provide an excellent opportunity for counting and talking about the number eight. Give each child a copy of page 16. Ask him to cut apart the shoes at the bottom of the page. Then have him count the dot set on one of the spider's legs. Have him glue the shoe with the corresponding numeral to the end of the leg. Have him continue until he's matched a shoe to each leg. Now that's some fancy footwork!

9

A Hairy, Not-So-Scary Spider
Counting, fine-motor skills

Mix a little math into small-group time when you have youngsters count out eight legs for this arachnid art activity! To prepare, purchase a large package of loose tea. Photocopy a simple spider head and body outline onto construction paper to make a class supply. Also gather several small glue bottles and old paintbrushes. First, have each child use crayons to draw a face on his spider outline. Next, have him squeeze glue onto the spider's body and spread it over the area with a paintbrush. Then have him squeeze eight lines of glue—four on each side of the spider's body—to represent the spider's eight legs. Give the child the tea leaves and invite him to take pinches of tea and sprinkle it all over the wet glue. Shake off the excess tea and observe the effect. Ooh—what a hairy-looking spider!

Curds and Whey Parfait
Following oral directions

So what exactly is curds and whey? The closest thing in your supermarket is cottage cheese! For a yummy and healthful snack, provide cottage cheese, well-drained diced peaches or crushed pineapple, and slices of maraschino cherries. Instruct each child to spoon a bit of cottage cheese into a clear plastic cup, followed by a spoonful of fruit. Repeat the layers and then complete this curds and whey parfait with—what else—a slice of cherry on top!

Patterns
Use with "Little Miss Muffet" on pages 5–10.

tuffet

Miss Muffet

spider

frightened Miss Muffet

A Web of *-at* Words

Cut.

Read.

Glue the *-at* words to the web.

©The Education Center, Inc. • *Once Upon a Nursery Rhyme* • TEC1113

pat	cat	tan	car
mat	far	sat	bat

Note to the teacher: Use with "Does That End in *-at?*" on page 8.

©The Education Center, Inc.

Name

Eight Great Legs

Cut.
Count.
Match.
Glue.

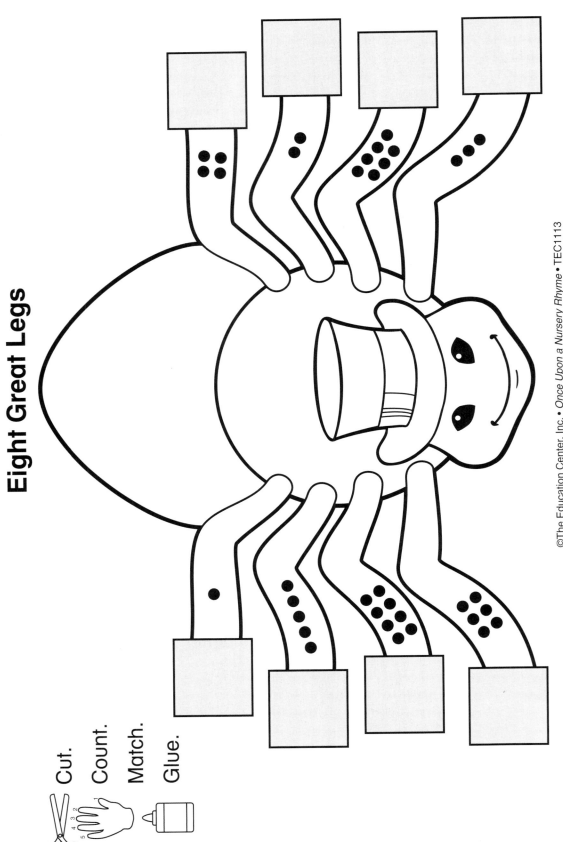

Note to the teacher: Use with "Eight Great Legs" on page 9.

16

Hey Diddle, Diddle

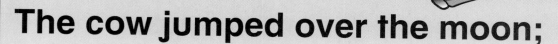

Hey diddle, diddle,

The cat and the fiddle,

The cow jumped over the moon;

The little dog laughed

To see such fun,

And the dish ran away with the spoon.

Hey Diddle, Diddle

Hey diddle, diddle,

The cat and the fiddle,

The cow jumped over the moon;

The little dog laughed

To see such fun,

And the dish ran away with the spoon.

Hey Diddle, Diddle

Youngsters will be over the moon about this collection of activities featuring the creative cast of characters from "Hey Diddle, Diddle"!

What Is a Fiddle?

Building on prior knowledge

Acquaint children with what a fiddle is before introducing "Hey Diddle, Diddle." Present the color cat-and-fiddle pattern. Then ask the children to explain what they think the cat is doing in the picture. Guide students to the conclusion that the cat is playing a musical instrument. Explain that the instrument is a fiddle (also called a violin), which is held under the chin and played with a bow. Have each child pretend to play a fiddle. Then play a recording of bluegrass music and prompt the children to play their imaginary fiddles each time they hear the instrument. Close this concert with a reading of "Hey Diddle, Diddle" using the poster on page 17.

/K/ Is for Cat!

Identifying beginning sounds /k/ and /d/

The little dog won't be the only one laughing when little ones change words in the nursery rhyme from familiar to funny! Ask youngsters to listen for words that begin with the /k/ sound as you slowly read the nursery rhyme poster on page 17. Once the words *cat* and *cow* have been identified, have students place the cat and cow patterns from page 24 into a pocket chart. Encourage children to name other words that begin with the /k/ sound. If desired, sketch a simple picture of each object on an index card and place it in the pocket chart. Then reread the nursery rhyme several times, each time replacing the words *cat* and *cow* with different words beginning with /k/. Repeat the steps with words that begin with the /d/ sound. The little *duck* laughed to see such fun!

Dishing Up Rhymes
Recognizing rhyming words

Instead of running away, the dish decides to stay to help make this kid-pleasing rhyme wheel! To prepare, make a copy of page 26 for each student. Gather a class supply of dessert-size paper plates (dishes). Cut a piece out of the side of each plate as shown. To begin, have each child color and cut out the picture cards. Direct her to stack the picture cards to make a booklet. Then have her staple them to the inside of a paper plate, opposite the prepared opening. Next, instruct her to place the plate on top of the rhyme wheel. Finally, help her secure it to the wheel by pushing a brad through the center of both pieces. As the youngster looks at each picture in the booklet, she turns the wheel to find the matching rhyme in the plate opening. Cat! Hat!

Marching Over the Moon!
Recognizing that words can show action

Youngsters will jump for joy in this action-packed review of the nursery rhyme! Have the children stand. Then recite the rhyme slowly and encourage students to act out the words *jumped, laughed,* and *ran* (be sure to tell children to run in place). Have the children act out the rhyme several times, replacing each action word with a different action (see suggestions below) for each repetition. Once the children understand the activity, have them suggest new action words to use in the rhyme. The dish *hopped* away with the spoon!

Action Words
hopped
marched
crawled
twirled
flew
tiptoed
walked
jogged
wiggled

20

Dish-and-Spoon Match

Matching letters, identifying the initial letter position in a word

Which spoon does the dish run away with? The spoon that has the matching letter! Invite youngsters to this dish-and-spoon center to match words by their beginning letters. In advance, enlarge the patterns on page 24. Cut out the patterns and glue each one to the inside of a dinner-size paper plate. Label each plate with the name of the cutout. Then use a permanent marker to write the beginning letter of each cutout name on the bowl of a plastic spoon.

To introduce the center, read each paper plate and discuss where the first letter in each word is located. Assist students in choosing the spoon that matches each letter. Then place the plates and spoons in the center for students to match independently. To extend the activity, use magazine pictures of common objects to make a different set of plates and spoons.

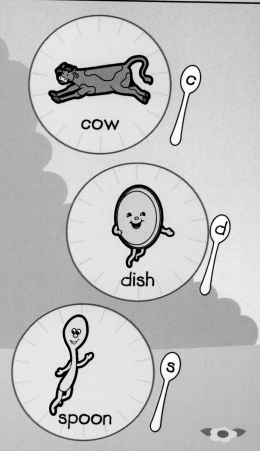

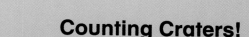

Counting Craters!

Counting, making a matching number set

Spot your little ones having fun when they make this jumping cow number book! To prepare, make five copies of page 28. Use a marker to draw a different number of moon craters (one to five) on each page. (To increase the skill level, replace the craters on each page with the written numeral). Make a copy of the pages for each child. Then staple each set to create a booklet. To begin the activity, give each child a booklet and access to a black ink stamp pad with washable ink. A youngster counts the number of craters on the moon. Then he places his index finger in the black ink and stamps that number of spots on the cow!

Moving Around the Moon

Using a prop to illustrate positional words

Provide plenty of positional word practice with these quick and easy cow and moon puppets! Enlarge the cow and moon patterns on page 24 and make a class supply. Have each child color and cut out one cow and one moon. Then help her tape a Popsicle stick to the back of each cutout to make a puppet. Have each student hold a puppet in each hand, with the cow puppet in her dominant hand. Encourage each youngster to move the cow puppet in relation to the moon puppet to demonstrate the positional words *over*, *under*, *beside*, *in front of*, *behind*, and *next to*.

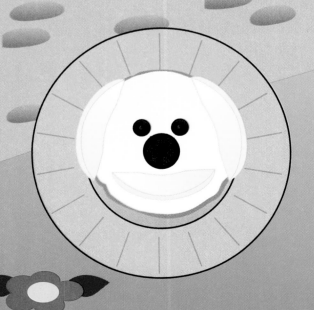

A Happy Hound

Developing fine-motor skills

Youngsters will want to "woof" down a tasty snack inspired by the rhyme's laughing dog! To make his snack, a student spreads cream cheese on an English muffin half. Next, he places two peeled, thinly sliced apple wedges (ears) on opposite sides of the English muffin. He adds two chocolate chip eyes and a Mini Oreo cookie nose. Then he places a thinly sliced apple wedge under the nose to create a smiling mouth. Hey diddle, delicious!

©The Education Center, Inc.

Patterns
Use with "Hey Diddle, Diddle" on pages 17–22.

cat and fiddle

dog

cow

dish

spoon

moon

cow

moon

dog

©The Education Center, Inc.

©The Education Center, Inc

©The Education Center, Inc.

Rhyme Wheel and Picture Cards

Use with "Dishing Up Rhymes" on page 20.

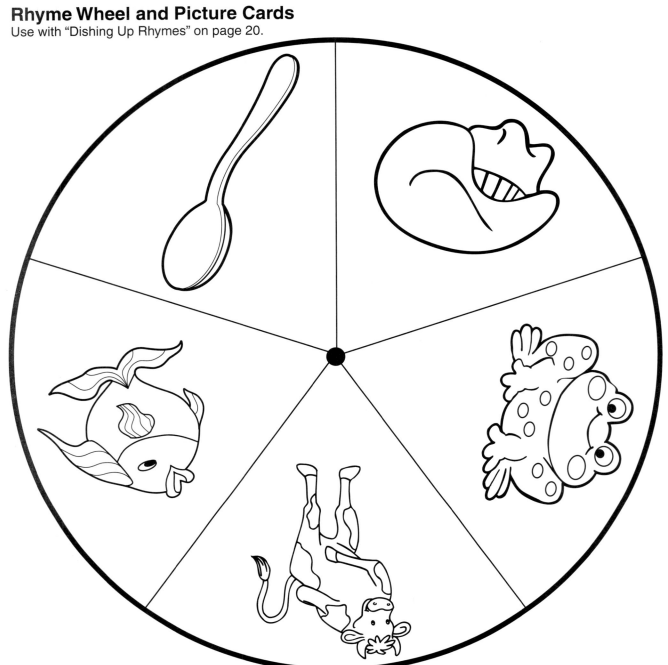

dish

spoon

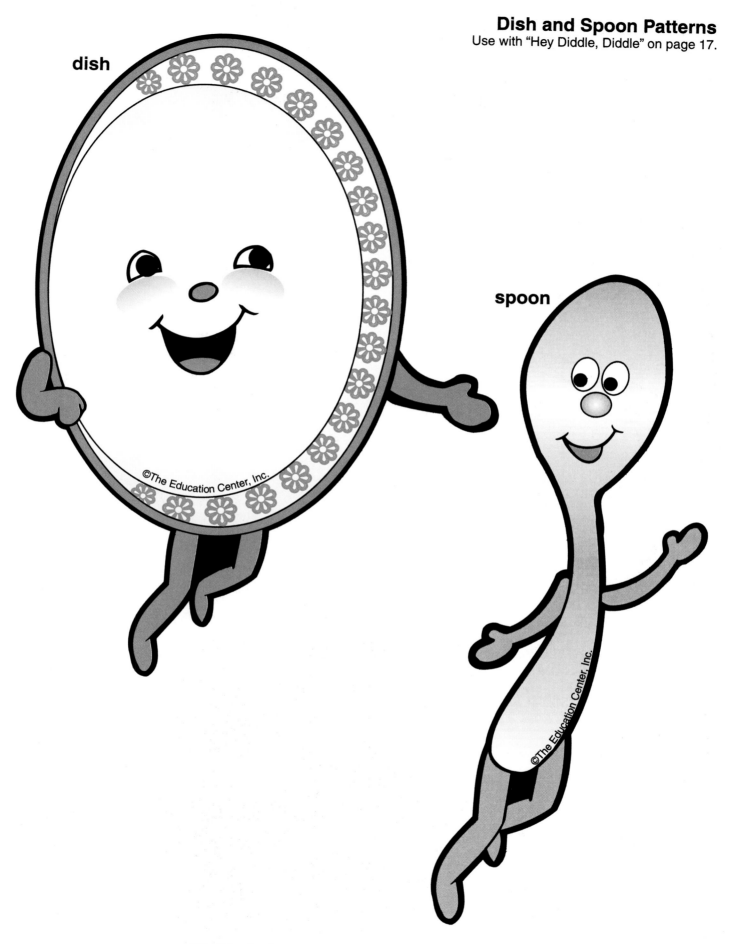

©The Education Center, Inc.

Note to the teacher: Use with "Counting Craters!" on page 21.

Twinkle, Twinkle, Little Star

Twinkle, twinkle, little star,

How I wonder what you are,

Up above the world so high,

Like a diamond in the sky.

Twinkle, twinkle, little star,

How I wonder what you are.

Twinkle, Twinkle, Little Star

Twinkle, twinkle, little star,

How I wonder what you are,

Up above the world so high,

Like a diamond in the sky.

Twinkle, twinkle, little star,

How I wonder what you are.

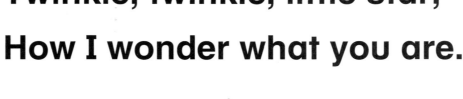

Twinkle, Twinkle Little Star

Twinkling stars are fascinating for young and old alike! Share this imaginative rhyme and accompanying activities with your little ones for a learning experience that's out of this world!

Starry Skies
Building on prior knowledge

Before introducing "Twinkle, Twinkle, Little Star," find out what your youngsters already know about stars. Ask students to describe stars and explain where they are in relation to Earth. Lead youngsters to establish that stars are very far away in space, and we can often see them when we stand outside at night. Next, invite each child to illustrate himself enjoying a starry sky with this simple art activity. Provide each child with a 12" x 18" sheet of black construction paper, a 2" x 12" strip of green construction paper, a cotton swab, access to a small cup of white paint, and a copy of the person pattern on page 38. Have each child glue the green paper strip to the bottom of his black paper to represent the ground. Next, have him dip one end of the swab into the paint and then dab it onto the black paper to resemble stars in the night sky. While the paint dries, encourage each child to color his pattern to look like himself. Then help him cut it out and glue it onto the page to complete the project. Mount the pictures on a black-covered bulletin board with the title "Twinkling Stars." Now that youngsters are familiar with starry skies, use the poster on page 29 and the accompanying patterns to introduce the rhyme. Twinkle, twinkle, little star, we know exactly where you are!

cat

Rhymes With *Star*
Discriminating between rhyming and nonrhyming words

This easy auditory activity will give your little ones plenty of practice with groups of rhyming words. To begin, recite the first two lines of the poem and point out that the words *star* and *are* rhyme because they end with the same sound. Next, say the words *star, are, bar,* and *cat;* then have a volunteer tell you which word in the group does not rhyme with the rest. Say another rhyming group, tucking in one word that doesn't rhyme. Which word does not belong? Continue saying groups of words in this fashion. Then, whenever you have a spare moment, revisit this activity. In no time you'll have a room full of rhyming stars!

31

Tap, Tap, Twinkle, Twinkle
Segmenting words

This segmenting activity will put a twinkle in your students' eyes and a rhythm in their step! In advance, make a wand from a tagboard copy of the star pattern on page 36. Decorate the star as desired; then use clear mailing tape to adhere it to a craft stick. Copy the rhyme onto a chart; then mount it in your group area. Invite a small group of students to softly recite the rhyme while you tap each syllable with the wand. Repeat the activity, this time inviting students to clap the syllables as you tap them. Then have student volunteers suggest other ways to note the syllables—such as marching, patting, and jumping—while you read and tap the rhyme. What fun!

Twinkle, Twinkle, Little Star

Twinkle, twinkle, little star,
How I wonder what you are,
Up above the world so high,
Like a diamond in the sky.
Twinkle, twinkle, little star,
How I wonder what you are.

That's a Match!
Matching words

Put some star power into print awareness with this activity! Laminate and display the poster and point to the word *wonder.* Ask your youngsters to search the poster for another occurence of that word; then have a volunteer point it out and circle it with a wipe-off pen. Next, invite students to examine the poster for other matching words. As each different volunteer points out a pair, check for understanding by having her explain how the words match. Then have her circle the pair. When all the matching words have been found, reread them with students. Then reinforce students' word-matching skills by giving each child a copy of page 40. Offer support as needed while each child cuts, matches, and glues the words. Encourage each child to take her completed sheet home to share with her family.

Sleepy Stars
Reciting and listening

Snuggle down for a rest with this cozy language activity. On a special day, arrange the tables in your room so students can rest underneath them. Next, sing the familiar lullaby version of the rhyme as your little ones get ready for rest time. When each child is tucked under a table, give him a small star sticker (glow-in-the-dark stars are especially fun). Invite him to softly chant or sing along with you as he sticks his star to the underside of the table. At the end of the rhyme, encourage him to think about his star as he drifts off to sleep. Sweet dreams!

Stellar Sets
Counting, comparing sets

Count on some stellar learning when your little ones practice creating and comparing sets. In advance, cut a class supply of four-inch squares from black construction paper. Store them in your small-group area with a supply of star stickers and a paper bag containing five magnetic numbers. Working with a group of five students, have each child, in turn, take a number from the bag and read it. Then give each child a paper square and enough stickers to match her number. Invite her to count aloud as she adheres her sticker(s) to her paper to make a set. When the sets are complete, ask two students to place theirs on the table for all to compare. Which set is larger? Which is smaller? Compare sets until each child has had a turn. What cool constellations!

Reach for a Star
Understanding opposites, movement

The stars are *up* in the sky and we are *down* here on Earth. Shine a spotlight on opposites with this musical movement activity! Invite students to sing the song while performing the accompanying movements. Repeat whenever spirits need lifting!

(sung to the tune of "This Old Man")

Stretch up, up.
Stretch up high!
Stretch to touch the starry sky.
Stretch right up, up, up,
  up so very far.
Look at every shining star!

Stand and stretch right arm overhead.
Stretch left arm overhead.
Stretch both arms overhead.
Stand on tiptoe; stretch both arms overhead
  and wiggle fingers.
Look up and wave arms.

Bend down, down.
Bend down low.
Bend to touch the earth below.
Bend right down, down, down, down
  and touch the ground.
Touch the green grass all around!

Bend slightly and extend right arm down.
Extend left arm down.
Bend; stretch both arms down.
Bend to touch fingertips to floor. Squat, touch
palms to floor, and look down.
Move palms around on floor.

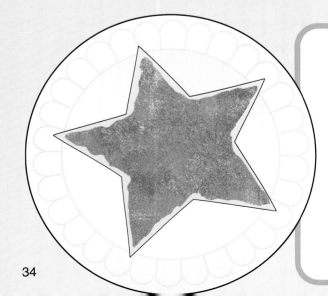

Sparkly Star Snacks
Following oral directions

Crunch, crunch, crunch—sweet stars we'll munch! Invite each child to use a cookie cutter to cut a star shape from a flour tortilla. Then help her place it on a cookie sheet, brush it with melted butter, and sprinkle it with cinnamon sugar. As students look on, bake the prepared stars at 350° for ten minutes or until golden brown and crispy. Let the stars cool; then serve them with cups of cold milk. How delicious!

©The Education Center, Inc.

Patterns

Use with "Twinkle, Twinkle, Little Star" on pages 29–34.

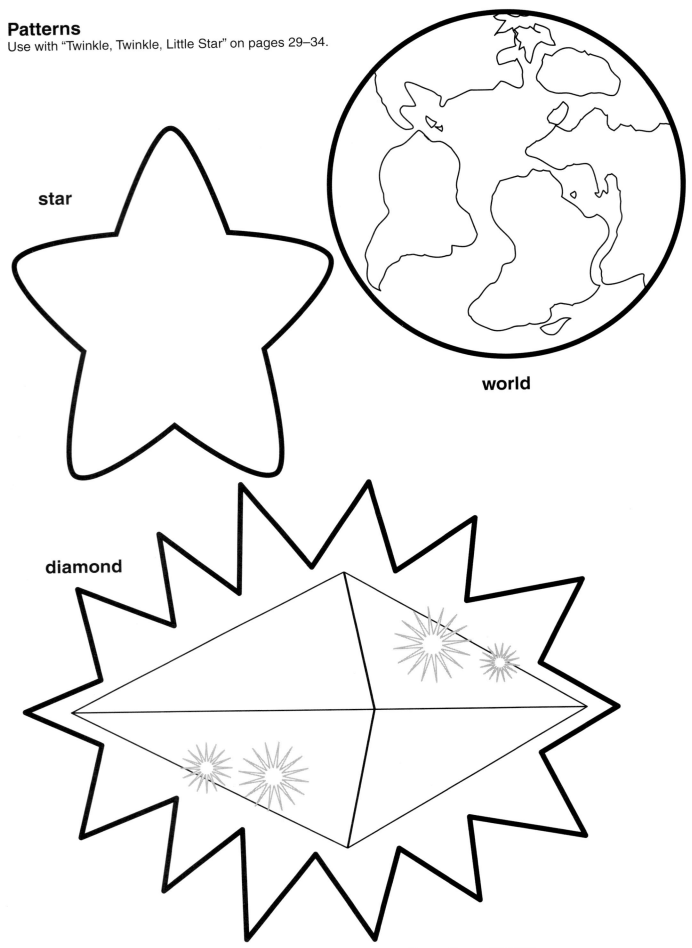

star

world

diamond

©The Education Center, Inc.

©The Education Center, Inc.

Name ______________________________

Star Power

Cut.

Match.

Glue.

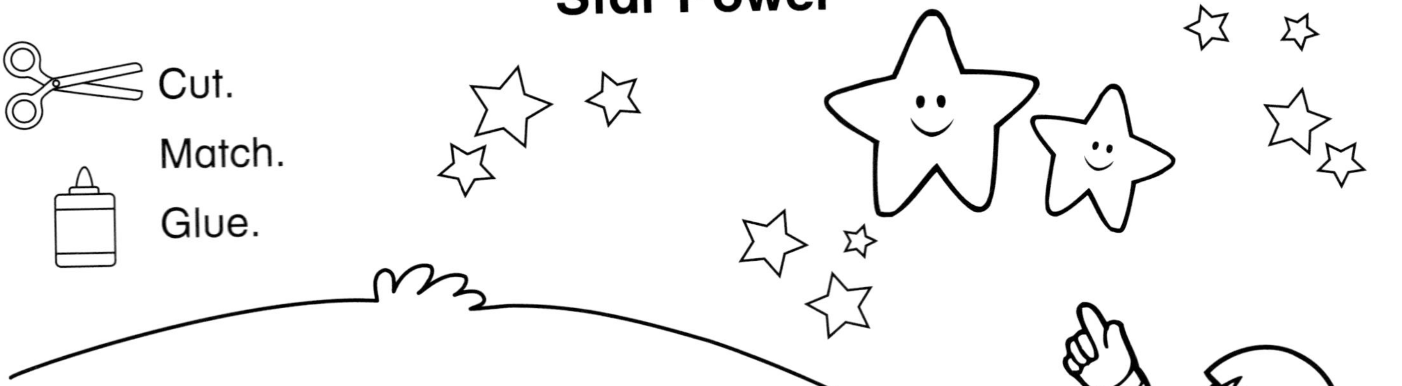

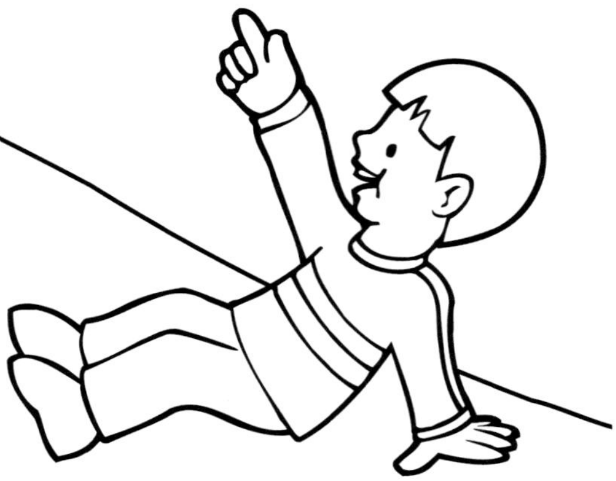

dog ☐ you ☐

ball ☐ car ☐ me ☐

and ☐ book ☐ go ☐

car	and	you	ball
book	go	dog	me

 Note to the teacher: Use with "That's a Match!" on page 32.

Jack Be Nimble

Jack be nimble;

Jack be quick.

Jack jump over

The candlestick.

Jack Be Nimble

Jack be nimble;

Jack be quick.

Jack jump over

The candlestick.

Jack Be Nimble

Ready for a rollicking good time? Then jump with Jack and enjoy this rhyme!

Up and Over!
Building on prior knowledge

How high can your students jump? Take them to the playground and find out! Begin by asking each child to demonstrate how high she can jump. Next, direct students to think of things they might jump over, such as lines drawn on the ground, sidewalk cracks, or beanbags. Explain that a person who can gracefully jump over things is said to be nimble. Invite each child to nimbly jump over a few items. To wrap up the activity, tell youngsters that they're going to hear about a boy named Jack who jumps over a candlestick. Then use the poster on page 41 and the accompanying character patterns to share the nursery rhyme.

Jumping Jacks and Jills
Segmenting words

Want to brighten syllable awareness? This activity will have your little ones jumping like Jack in no time! To prepare, copy each word of the rhyme onto a different card and then place the cards in a pocket chart. Slowly read the rhyme, clapping the syllables of each word as you go. Then read the rhyme again, inviting students to clap and recite with you. Choose one word card and read it aloud. Prompt students to notice whether the word is long or short, and to predict how many syllables it has. Ask a student volunteer to repeat the word and "jump" the syllables. Continue in this manner with several volunteers and words. Then get the wiggles out by having everyone recite and jump the rhyme. All together now! "Jack be nim-ble!"

43

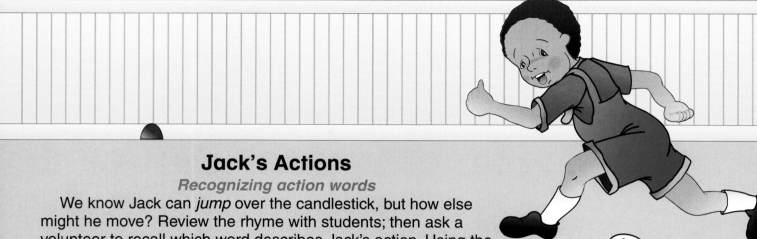

Jack's Actions
Recognizing action words

We know Jack can *jump* over the candlestick, but how else might he move? Review the rhyme with students; then ask a volunteer to recall which word describes Jack's action. Using the word cards from "Jumping Jacks and Jills" on page 43, place the phrase "Jack jump over the candlestick" in a pocket chart. Read the phrase aloud, paying special attention to the word *jump.* Lay an enlarged copy of the candlestick pattern (page 48) on the floor and invite a student volunteer to demonstrate jumping over it. Next, suggest that there are other ways to move over a candle-stick. Encourage students to supply additional action words—such as *leap, hop,* and *step*—as you program an index card with each new word. Then use one to replace *jump* in the chart. Read the phrase aloud, inviting a student volunteer to model the new action. Continue the activity in this same manner, substituting the word *jump* with different action words. Jack *leap* over the candlestick!

Quick, Quick Candlestick
Identifying -ick word spellings

Help your youngsters get a jump on looking for word spellings! Show young-sters the words *quick* and *candlestick;* then ask whether anyone notices something interesting about the two words. Lead students to conclude that the words end with the same series of letters. Explain that these letters are pronounced /ick/, and ask students to brainstorm other *-ick* words while you record responses on the board. Encourage students to help you check each suggested word for the *-ick* spelling, and erase any that do not fit the pattern. Praise your youngsters' efforts and follow up by giving each child a copy of page 50. Have each child look at the words and then color each word that ends in *-ick.* Great job!

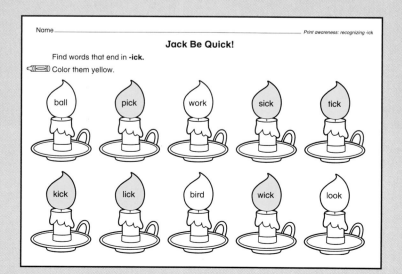

Name _____

Jack Be Quick!

Print awareness: recognizing -ick

Find words that end in **-ick.**

Color them yellow.

| ball | pick | work | sick | tick |
| kick | lick | bird | wick | look |

44

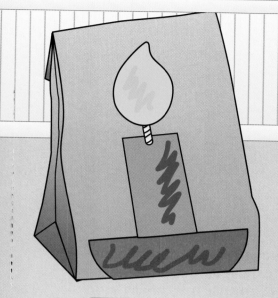

Positional Word Workout
Recognizing positional words

Why just jump over a candlestick when you can sit beside it, walk away from it, and hop toward it too? In advance, duplicate the patterns on page 52 to make a class supply. Give one set to each child and ask her to color the patterns and cut them out. Have her glue the cutouts to a paper lunch bag. If desired, invite each child to glue a white yarn wick between the candle and flame. When the glue is dry, direct her to open the bag and stuff a crumpled sheet of newspaper inside. Help her fold over the top of the bag and staple it closed.

Have youngsters stand in a circle with their candles on the floor in front of them. Give a movement direction that contains a positional word or phrase, such as "Walk around your candle." (See the list for more suggestions.) Then prompt each child to follow your directions. Go ahead—get moving!

Positional Phrases
Hop beside
Put your foot under
Put your hand over
Stand behind
Sit in front of
Skip away from
Tiptoe toward

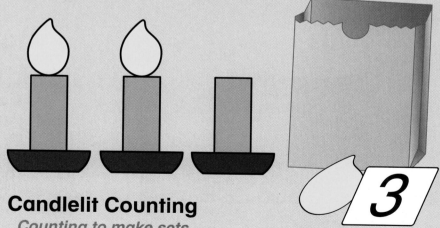

Candlelit Counting
Counting to make sets

A candle isn't complete without a flame to top it off! Invite students to "light" paper candles with faux flames as they practice making sets. Make ten construction paper copies of the patterns on page 52. Cut out the pieces and then glue the candles to the candlesticks. Laminate the prepared candles and flames for durability. Store all the pieces in your math center with a paper bag containing number cards labeled 1–10. Invite a child in this center to select a card, read the number, and "light" that many candles with paper flames. Have her count and make several more sets in this same manner. Your youngsters will positively glow with success!

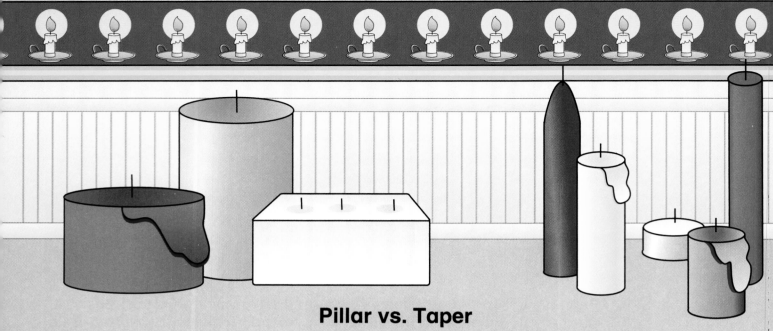

Pillar vs. Taper
Sorting and classifying

Shed a little light on attributes with this small-group activity. In advance, request dona-tions of used candles in various shapes, sizes, and colors. As candles arrive, arrange them on a table and encourage students to study them. Next, have each child in a small group select a candle and examine it closely. Invite her to describe her candle's color, thickness, shape, and appearance. Lead students to conclude that candles have many attributes, or distinguishing factors. Next, have students choose two attributes (such as wide and not wide) and sort the candles into those groups. Then have youngsters choose another set of attributes and sort again. How many ways can your students sort the candles?

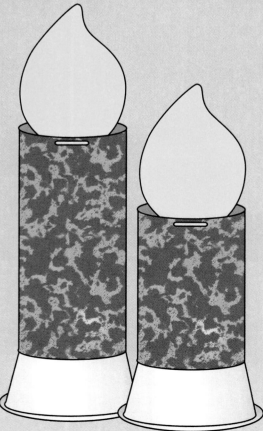

Candle Seriation
Ordering objects by size

Create a set of paper tube candles to use in a size seriation center. Cut paper towel and toilet tissue tubes into eight lengths of varying sizes. Sponge-paint the tubes so that they all match. Then make eight yellow construction paper copies of the flame pattern on page 52. Cut out each flame and staple it to a different tube. Then glue the bottom of each tube to a white paper bathroom cup to resemble a candlestick as shown. Put the completed candles in a center. Invite a child in this center to compare the candles and then stand them in order from longest to shortest. Illuminating!

©The Education Center, Inc.

Patterns
Use with "Jack Be Nimble" on pages 41–46.

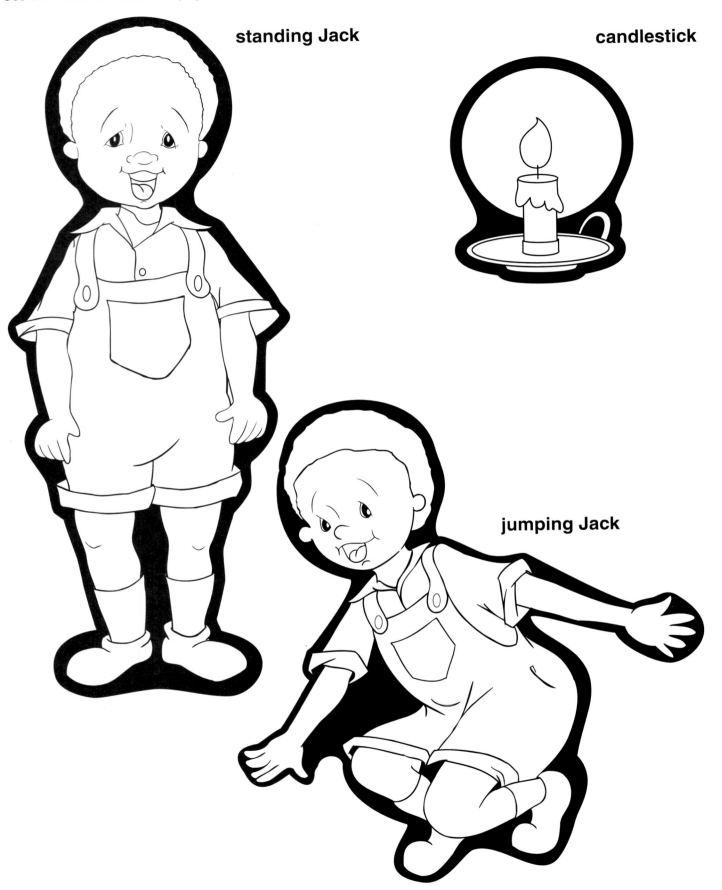

standing Jack

candlestick

jumping Jack

Name _____

50

Jack Be Quick!

Find words that end in -ick.

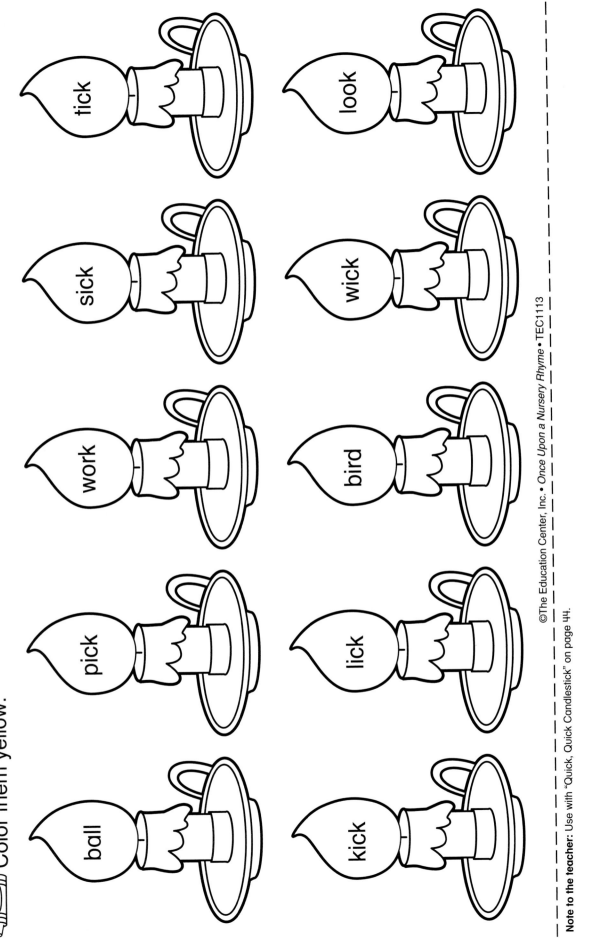

Color them yellow.

tick

look

sick

wick

work

bird

pick

lick

ball

kick

©The Education Center, Inc. • *Once Upon a Nursery Rhyme* • TEC1113

Note to the teacher: Use with "Quick, Quick Candlestick" on page 44.

Patterns

Use with "Positional Word Workout" and "Candlelit Counting" on page 45 and "Candle Seriation" on page 46.

candlestick

flame

candle

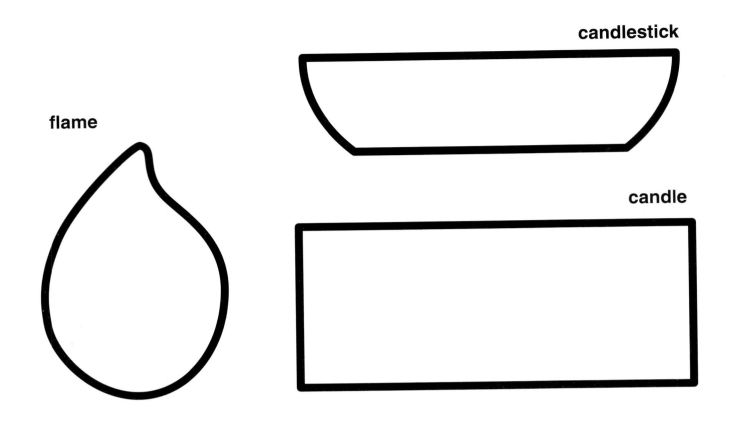

- -

candlestick

flame

candle

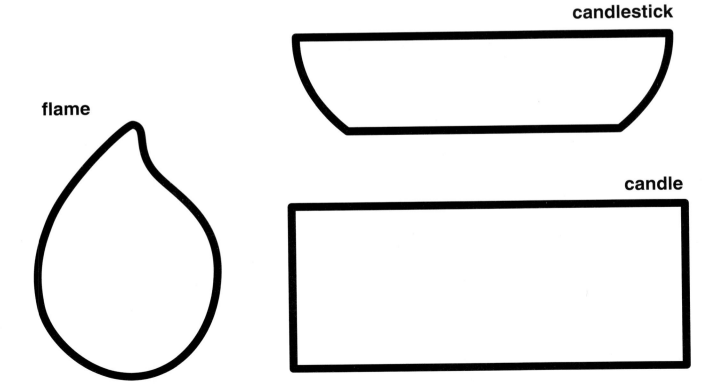

©The Education Center, Inc. • *Once Upon a Nursery Rhyme* • TEC1113

Little Boy Blue

Little Boy Blue,

Come blow your horn.

The sheep's in the meadow.

The cow's in the corn.

Where is the boy

Who looks after the sheep?

He's under a haystack,

Fast asleep.

Little Boy Blue

Little Boy Blue,

Come blow your horn.

The sheep's in the meadow.

The cow's in the corn.

Where is the boy

Who looks after the sheep?

He's under a haystack,

Fast asleep.

Little Boy Blue

A long nap and some adventurous livestock make for a day Little Boy Blue won't soon forget! So invite your youngsters to pull up a haystack for a bundle of activities straight from this memorable nursery rhyme!

Familiar With Farms
Building on prior knowledge

Help youngsters become familiar with farm-related vocabulary with an imaginary field trip to the country! Invite children to discuss any experiences they may have had visiting or living in a rural area. Then take students on an imaginary field trip. Have youngsters pretend to walk through a meadow, feel the cool grass, and listen to the crickets. Encourage them to run in place and pretend they are running through the long rows of a cornfield. Finally, invite the children to pet pretend farm animals before leaning against an imaginary haystack for a nice long nap! This farm is a fascinating place!

Word Pairs
sleep, sheep
pig, cat
cow, plow
toy, boy
hay, play
cup, pup
blue, glue
pet, jet

A Corn Horn
Recognizing rhyming words

Little ones get to blow their own horns when they identify rhyming words with these fanciful corn horns! To prepare, make two copies of the corn pattern on page 62 for each child. Then cut a class supply of 9" x 9" yellow construction paper squares. To make a horn, help each child roll and then tape a piece of prepared construction paper into a funnel shape. Assist the student in trimming the funnel to resemble a horn. Next, instruct her to color and cut out the corn patterns. Have each child glue a cut-out to each side of the horn. Allow time for the glue to dry. Finally, say pairs of words (see the suggestions shown) and then instruct children to "blow" on their horns briefly if the words rhyme. Corn! Horn!

Everybody Say, "Hay!"
Segmenting words

Youngsters discover that words can be segmented into smaller parts with help from this haystack puppet! To make the puppet, copy page 64 onto yellow construction paper. Cut out the patterns; then glue them to a paper lunch bag as shown. Next, divide the students into two groups. Put on the haystack puppet. Then explain that the puppet needs help breaking large words into smaller parts. Have the puppet "say" the word *haystack.* Encourage one group of children to say "hay" and then the other group to say "stack." Continue the activity with each compound from the word list shown.

Word List
cornfield
butterfly
pancake
cowboy
sandpaper
ladybug
bedtime
firefly
notebook
eyelid

Little Boy Blue's *B* Book
Identifying the letter B

What else is hidden under the haystack? A bunch of items that begin with *B!* Invite little ones to identify the letter *B* when they make this lift-the-flap booklet! Staple five 6" x 9" pieces of blue construction paper together to make a booklet for each child. Next, gather the supplies listed below and then guide each child through the directions to complete her booklet.

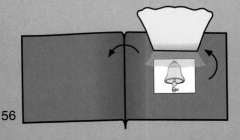

Materials for each child:
6 yellow construction paper copies of the haystack pattern on page 62
copy of page 65

Directions:
1. Cut out each haystack.
2. Glue the top edge of a haystack to the front cover and to each booklet page to create a flap. Allow time for the glue to dry.
3. Color and cut out the booklet title and picture cards.
4. Glue the booklet title to the haystack on the front cover; then glue the Little Boy Blue card under the haystack.
5. Glue each remaining picture card under a different haystack. Allow time for the glue to dry.
6. Write your name on the front cover.
7. Circle the *b*'s found in the words under the haystacks.

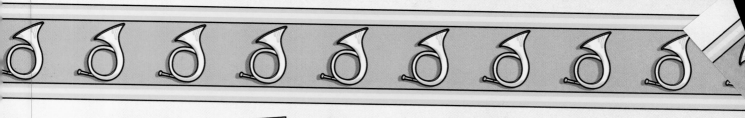

How Many Stalks Are Standing?

	3
	1
	4
	2
	5

Cows in the Cornfield!

Counting

When cows get loose in a cornfield, they make a terrible mess eating and trampling the corn! Have little ones use counting skills to find out how many cornstalks are left standing after a visit from the cows. Give each child a copy of page 66. Then have him color the page and cut out the numbers. Encourage each student to count the number of cornstalks left in each row and then glue the number in the appropriate box. Looks like a lot of cleanup for Little Boy Blue!

Sweet Dreams

Writing to complete a sentence

Why didn't Little Boy Blue wake up and blow his horn? He must have been in the middle of a wonderful dream! Invite your youngsters to write and illustrate a dream for Little Boy Blue to make this wall display. In advance, tape a large haystack-shaped piece of yellow bulletin board paper to a wall. Enlarge a copy of Little Boy Blue from page 60. Then color and cut out the pattern. Tape the pattern to the bottom of the haystack. Next, program a 9" x 12" sheet of white paper for each child with the dream bubble and sentence starter shown. To begin the activity, instruct each student to draw a picture of a happy dream for Little Boy Blue in the bubble. Then have her complete the sentence (or dictate a sentence) to explain the picture. Have each child cut out her dream bubble. Tape each bubble to the wall display above Little Boy Blue, adding extra paper circles where necessary. That's a dreamy display!

Little Boy Blue is dreamimg about...
cows in the barn.

A Haystack Snack
Developing fine-motor skills
The horn on top of this haystack snack is the crowning touch! To make his snack, a youngster spreads chocolate frosting on a Ritz cracker. Then he places a spoonful of chow mein noodles on top of the frosting to resemble a haystack. Finally, he tops the haystack with a Bugles corn snack to represent Little Boy Blue's horn. Yum!

Corn Prints
Using printing to give the appearance of texture
Leave an impression on little ones with this creative corn-print painting. To prepare, gather and shuck four ears of corn. Personalize for each child a large oval pattern on a sheet of 12" x 18" white construction paper. Then place a thin layer of yellow paint in a shallow tray. To begin the activity, invite a group of up to four children to your painting area. Have each child grasp the ends of an ear of corn, roll it in the paint, and then roll the corn across the piece of prepared paper. Allow time for the paint to dry. Then have each student cut out his oval. Next, instruct each child to crumple and then straighten four green tissue paper strips. Have him glue the strips to the oval to make an ear of corn with husks. Display the ears on a bulletin board with enlarged copies of the cow pattern from page 60. There are cows in this cornfield!

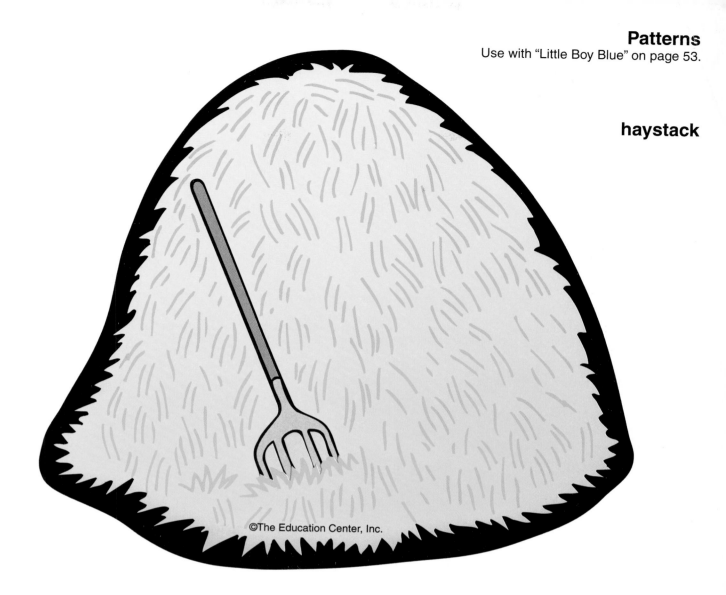

haystack

Little Boy Blue

©The Education Center, Inc.

Patterns
Use with "Little Boy Blue" on pages 53–58.

haystack

Little Boy Blue

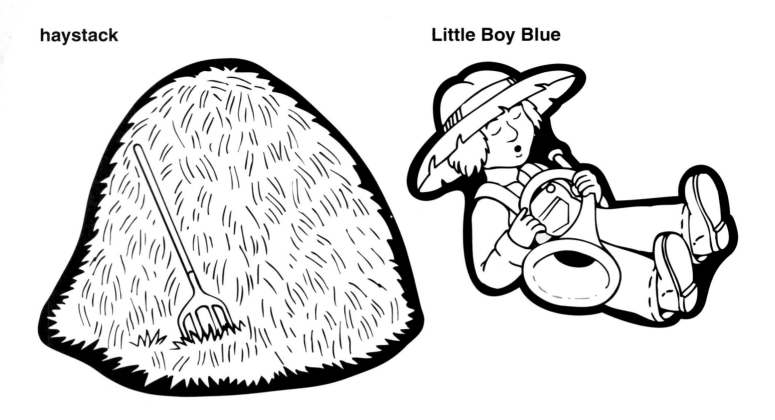

cow in the corn

sheep in the meadow

©The Education Center, Inc.

©The Education Center, Inc.

Corn Pattern
Use with "A Corn Horn" on page 55.

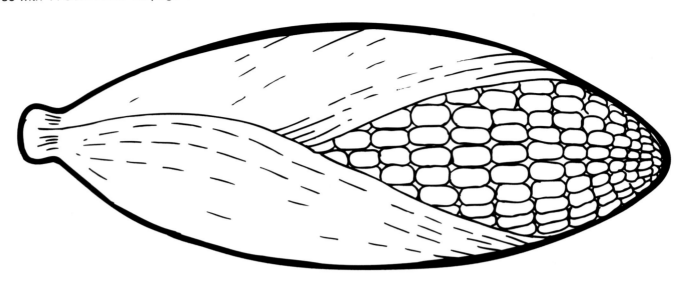

Haystack Pattern
Use with "Little Boy Blue's *B* Book" on page 56.

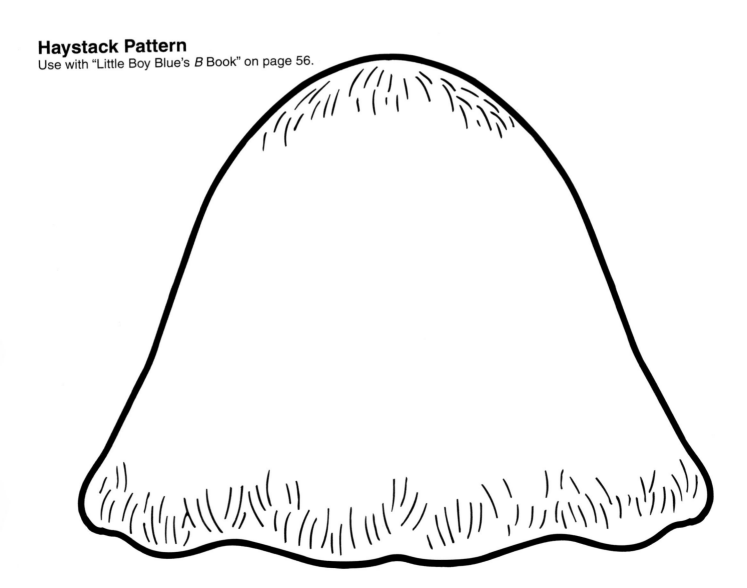

©The Education Center, Inc.

Haystack Puppet Pattern
Use with "Everybody Say, 'Hay!'" on page 56.

Little Boy Blue's *B* Book

by _____

Little Boy Blue

bell

book

ball

bug

How Many Stalks Are Standing?

1   2   3   4   5

Note to the teacher: Use with "Cows in the Cornfield!" on page 57.

Humpty Dumpty

Humpty Dumpty sat on a wall.

Humpty Dumpty had a great fall.

All the king's horses

And all the king's men

Couldn't put Humpty together again.

Humpty Dumpty

Humpty Dumpty sat on a wall.

Humpty Dumpty had a great fall.

All the king's horses

And all the king's men

Couldn't put Humpty together again.

Humpty Dumpty

All the king's horses and all the king's men couldn't prevent your little ones from having fun with everyone's favorite egghead, Humpty Dumpty!

Introducing Eggs
Building on prior knowledge

Gather students in your circle area and show them an egg. Where have they seen one of these before? Guide students to tell how they have seen eggs cooked. Next, bring out a clear bowl. Ask a student volunteer to crack the egg on the side of the bowl. Talk about what the inside of the egg looks like compared to the outside. Then ask the child who cracked the egg to put it back together. When the student hesitates, begin a discussion about why a cracked egg can't be reassembled. Next, seal the eggshell in a plastic bag, pass it around, and have students feel how fragile it is. Then tell students that they'll be learning a rhyme about an egg that breaks and can't be fixed. Continue by using the poster on page 67 and accompanying patterns to introduce "Humpty Dumpty" for the first time.

Rhyme and Pass
Supplying rhyming words

Seat your little ones in a circle for this rhyming activity hosted by Humpty himself! In advance, cut out and laminate the Humpty Dumpty color pattern on page 73. Show the cutout to the class and then repeat the rhyme below. Using the cutout as a puppet, have Humpty Dumpty name a word, such as *sat*. Pass Humpty to the child next to you and encourage her to give a rhyming word, such as *pat*. She then passes the cutout to the next child, who says another rhyming word. After several rhymes, repeat the rhyme below and have Humpty supply a new word from a different word family to continue the game.

Humpty Dumpty is here today,
And this is what he has to say:
"I'll say a word, and you say a rhyme.
Bet you can do it every time!"

Putting an Egg Together
Blending

Unlike Humpty Dumpty, the eggs in this activity can be put back together again! Putting them together will help your youngsters practice blending sounds to make words. Demonstrate for a small group by holding one half of a plastic egg in each hand. Choose a simple two-phoneme word from the rhyme, such as *men*. Hold up one half of the egg and say the onset—/m/. Then hold up the other half and say the rime—/en/. Push the two halves together as you slowly say the whole word—*men*. Next, give each child his own egg and have everyone try blending the sounds of other simple words with you. Wrap up the activity by giving each child a word to blend on his own. It's a shame this wouldn't have worked for poor old Humpty!

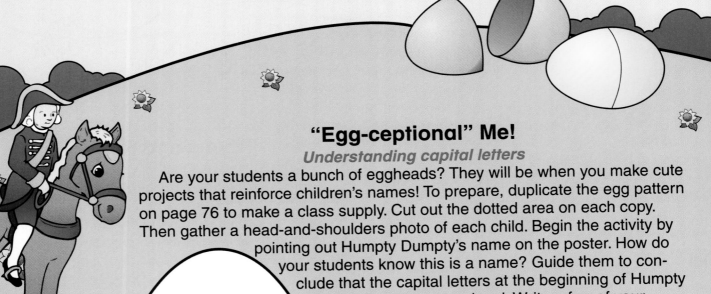

"Egg-ceptional" Me!
Understanding capital letters

Are your students a bunch of eggheads? They will be when you make cute projects that reinforce children's names! To prepare, duplicate the egg pattern on page 76 to make a class supply. Cut out the dotted area on each copy. Then gather a head-and-shoulders photo of each child. Begin the activity by pointing out Humpty Dumpty's name on the poster. How do your students know this is a name? Guide them to conclude that the capital letters at the beginning of Humpty Dumpty's name are a signal. Write a few of your student's names on the board and point out the capital letters at the beginning of each one. Then give each child her photo and an egg pattern. Have her cut out the egg and then position her photo so that her face shows through the cutout area. Help her tape the photo in place on the back of the egg. Use a light marker, such as a highlighter, to write the child's name below her photo. Then ask her to use a dark marker to trace over the capital letter at the beginning of her name. Display the finished egghead portraits on a bulletin board. Now that's a capital idea!

Nancy

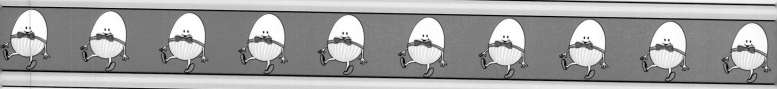

Act It Out!
Retelling a story

Your budding actors will enjoy taking turns playing the part of the hapless Humpty when your group acts out this simple rhyme. In advance, make an easy mask for Humpty Dumpty to wear. Cut a large egg shape from a sheet of 9" x 12" white construction paper. Lay a small paper plate in the center of the egg shape, trace around it, and then cut out the circle. Staple a length of sentence strip to each side of the opening; then fit the egg headband onto a child's head and staple the strip ends together.

Invite one child to play Humpty and a few others to play the roles of the king's horses and men. Have the class recite the rhyme as Humpty sits and then falls off a wall (a low stool or milk crate). Encourage the king's horses and men to rush to Humpty's aid at the appropriate point and to wear their saddest looks as Humpty continues to lie on the floor. Then repeat the rhyme until everyone has had a turn to play a part!

A Dozen Dumpties
Matching numbers 1–12

Maybe Humpty Dumpty is forever broken, but the eggs at this center can certainly be put back together again and again and again! To prepare, gather 12 plastic eggs, an empty egg carton, and a black permanent marker. Break an egg into its two halves and then use the marker to label both halves "1." Continue in this manner with the rest of the eggs until each is labeled with a different number from 1 to 12. Place the "broken" eggs into a large resealable plastic bag; then store the bag and carton in your math center. Have a student in this center find the egg halves with matching numerals, reassemble the eggs, and place them in the egg carton. After you've checked her work, have her break the eggs apart and store them in the bag for the next child to use.

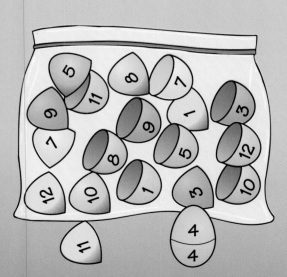

71

Horses and Men

One-to-one correspondence

All the king's horses and all the king's men will help you teach math skills again and again! Make a class supply of the reproducible on page 78. Have each child color and then cut out the men at the bottom of the page. Ask her to glue one man onto each horse. When students have completed their sheets, ask questions such as the following to help develop more math skills: Are there more men with horses or without? How many more horses would be needed so that each man could have one?

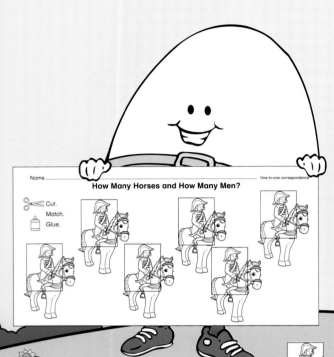

Name _____ One-to-one correspondence
How Many Horses and How Many Men?
✂ Cut.
Match.
Glue.

No More Climbing on the Wall, Please!

Dictating a letter

For a fine follow-up to this classic nursery rhyme, have youngsters think of ways Humpty could have prevented his fateful fall. After rereading the rhyme, invite your class to help you write a letter to Humpty Dumpty. Ask the class to dictate reasons why climbing on the high wall is a bad idea and how Humpty could have made safer decisions. Post the completed letter in your classroom. Safe and sound!

Dear Humpty Dumpty,
    Please don't ever climb on that high wall again! It's not safe to climb on walls. You could have held a grown-up's hand. It would have been better to stay on the ground. You could have worn a helmet to keep your head safe. We wear helmets when we ride bikes. We are sad you got hurt. We love you!

                    Your friends,
                    Mrs. Goren's class

Humpty Dumpty

©The Education Center, Inc.

wall

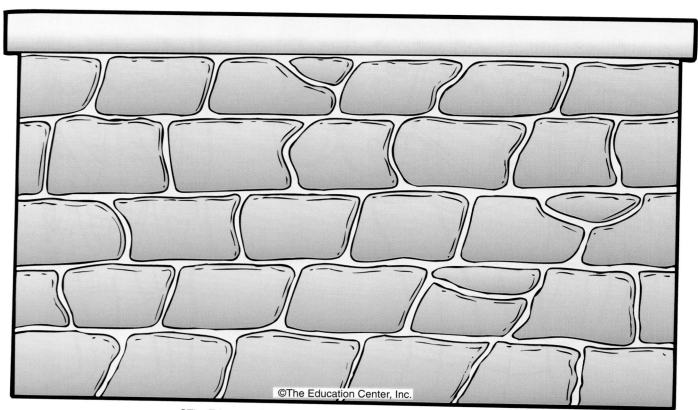

©The Education Center, Inc.

Patterns
Use with "Humpty Dumpty" on pages 67–72.

Humpty Dumpty

wall

broken Humpty Dumpty

king's horses

king's men

74   ©The Education Center, Inc. • *Once Upon a Nursery Rhyme* • TEC1113

©The Education Center, Inc.

Egg Pattern

Use with "'Egg-ceptional' Me!" on page 70.

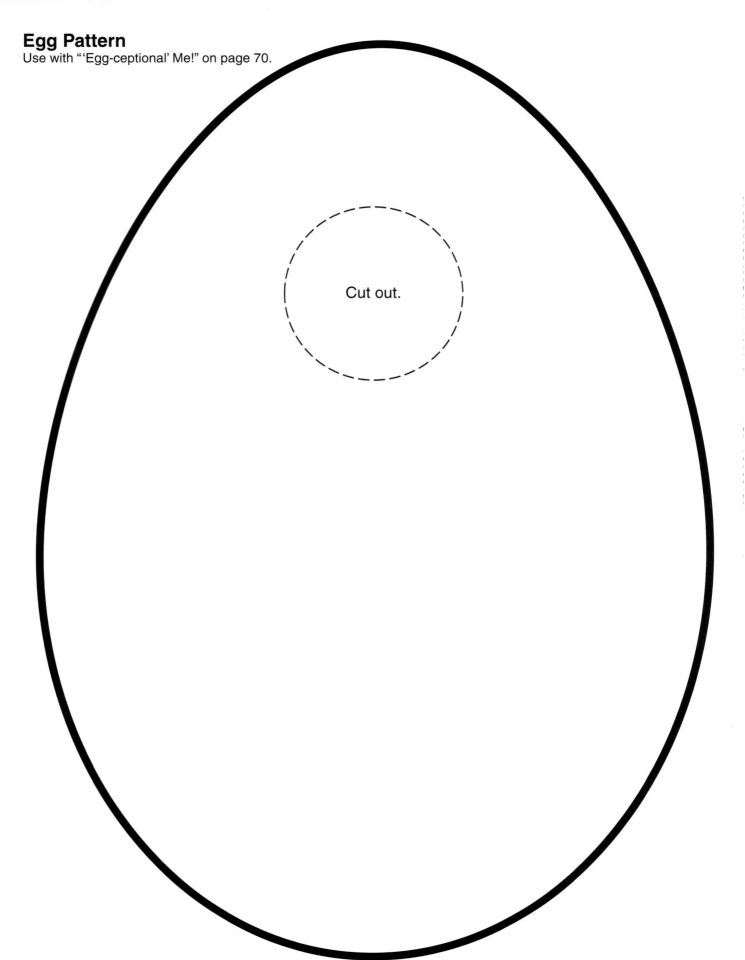

Cut out.

king's horses

king's men

Name _____

How Many Horses and How Many Men?

Cut.

Match.

Glue.

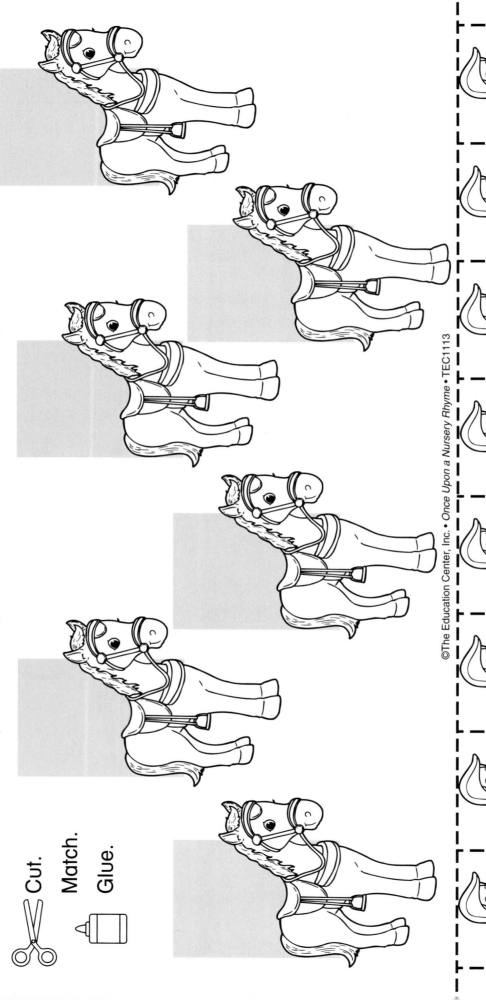

Note to the teacher: Use with "Horses and Men" on page 72.

Jack and Jill

Jack and Jill went up the hill
To fetch a pail of water;
Jack fell down and broke his crown,
And Jill came tumbling after.

Jack and Jill

Jack and Jill went up the hill

To fetch a pail of water;

Jack fell down and broke his crown,

And Jill came tumbling after.

Jack and Jill

Who knew that Jack and Jill's spill on a hill could lead to so much learning? Use the ideas in this unit to help your youngsters learn about rhyming, opposites, and much, much more!

Simon Says, "Fetch!"
Building on prior knowledge

Play a game of Simon Says to reinforce the meanings of the words *fetch* and *crown*. To begin, ask students, "What would you do if I asked you to fetch a crayon?" Then lead youngsters to discuss the meaning of the word *fetch* (to bring back). Then give students several more commands incorporating the word *fetch* to build their understanding of the word. Next, change the format of the game slightly to include the word *crown* in commands such as "Simon says, 'Hold a crayon above your crown.'" Discuss with students the meaning of the word *crown* (the top of the head). Continue play to reinforce the meaning of each word. Then have youngsters listen carefully for the words *fetch* and *crown* as you use the poster on page 79 and accompanying patterns to introduce the rhyme "Jack and Jill." Simon says, "Good job!"

Hold a crayon above your crown.

ROCK!

/k/	/l/
Jack	Jill
stick	full
rock	hall
pick	bell
block	mall
trick	shell
clock	small
sock	well

Thumbs Up
Recognizing ending sounds /k/ and /l/

Little ears will tune in to ending sounds in words during this activity. Share the color Jack and Jill patterns with students. Discuss the sound heard at the end of each character's name. Then display the Jack pattern. Tell students that you will say a list of words (see the suggestions at the left) and that some of them will end with the /k/ sound (as at the end of Jack) and some will end differently. Instruct each child to show you a thumbs-up if a word ends with the /k/ sound and a thumbs-down if it doesn't. Then repeat the activity, using the Jill pattern and a new list of words to focus on the /l/ sound. This activity is quick and simple!

A Pail of Sounds
Counting letter sounds

Make sure your youngsters have their listening ears on for this sound-counting lesson! To prepare, gather the color patterns of Jack walking, Jill walking, the pail, and the well, plus a child's sand pail. Give each child in a small group a supply of DUPLO blocks. Show students one of the patterns and say the character's or object's name. Then have each student count the sounds they hear in the name as you repeat it slowly. Instruct him to place that number of blocks in a stack. Repeat the word once again, directing each child to touch a block in his stack as he hears each sound. After the exercise, invite each youngster to put his stack of sounds in the pail before moving to the next pattern name. *Pail* has three sounds!

Jill
drill
bill
grill
hill
spill
Jack
rack
sack
tack
track
black

A Word Family Reunion
Matching words to word families

Your little ones will help word families reunite with this rime-grouping activity! To prepare, write each of the words from the list shown on a different index card. Display the cards in a pocket chart and then read each one to students. Discuss the similarities in the word endings and explain that words with endings that sound the same belong to the same word family. Next, shuffle the cards and then tell students that they will pretend to be words in a word family. Give each child a card and read the word on it to her. After all of the cards have been distributed, instruct each student to hold her card in front of her and repeatedly say her word as she moves around the room. Have students listen for other children saying words with the same ending as their own. Instruct youngsters to group themselves together with others whose words have the same word ending. After the groups have been formed, have each child say her word to check for accuracy. What a nice word family reunion!

A "Well-th" of Opposites
Identifying opposites

Dip into opposites with these cute little booklets! To prepare, make a class set of the booklet pages on pages 88 and 90. Gather two craft sticks and a 3½-inch construction paper square for each child. Give each student a copy of pages 88 and 90. Instruct him to write his name on the booklet cover where indicated. Have him color and cut out the booklet cover and pages and the opposites cards. Direct him to glue a card to each booklet page to make an opposites pair. When the glue is dry, help each child stack his pages in order behind his cover. Then staple each booklet along the left side. Next, give each student two craft sticks and a construction paper square. Have him glue one end of each stick to the back of his booklet as shown. When the glue is dry, have the child fold his paper square in half and add a dab of glue to the top of each stick. Help each child position his folded paper so that the glue will adhere to the paper's crease as shown. Finally, pair students and have them share their "well-th" of opposites.

Varying Volumes
Comparing volumes

Little ones will love fetching a few pails of water for this outdoor activity! In advance, collect three small pails, each of a different size. Also gather three large clear containers of the same size. Have students position the pails in order from smallest to largest and label each as shown. Next, instruct three student volunteers to fill the pails with water. Help students pour the water from each pail into a different clear container and then compare the water levels in each one. Do your students need to rethink the order in which the pails were placed? If so, have youngsters reposition the pails. Sometimes looks can be deceiving!

First-Aid Friends

Learning proper care for cuts

Jack has broken his crown! Is there a doctor available to help? You'll have a roomful of little doctors after this lesson on bandaging injuries! Prior to the activity, cut several long lengths of white crepe paper streamer (bandages) and dampen several paper towels. Discuss with students the importance of cleaning a cut or scrape and then applying a bandage. Next, place the bandages, paper towels, and several dolls (patients) at a center. Have each little doctor select a patient, clean its "injury" with a damp paper towel, and then wrap the injury with a bandage. The dolly patients in your classroom are sure to be well cared for!

It's All Downhill!

Experimenting with acceleration

We know that Jack and Jill fell down a hill. Let's take that idea a step further and have students test acceleration speeds on ramps made from a board and books. Explain to students that a ball's speed will increase as it rolls down a ramp. Then place a book on the floor and position a board on it to create a ramp. Release a ball at the top of the ramp and have students observe it as it rolls to the bottom. Repeat this demonstration, adding more books to the stack on the floor each time. Lead students to conclude that the higher the ramp, the greater the speed at which the ball travels. Then allow students to experiment with their own ramps and a ball. Your little ones will be inclined to try this activity again and again!

Patterns

Use with "Jack and Jill" on page 79, "Thumbs Up" on page 81, and "A Pail of Sounds" on page 82.

Jack walking

©The Education Center, Inc.

©The Education Center, Inc.

Jill walking

Patterns

Use with "Jack and Jill" on pages 79–84.

Jack tumbling

Jill tumbling

pail

Jack walking

Jill walking

well

©The Education Center, Inc.

©The Education Center, Inc.

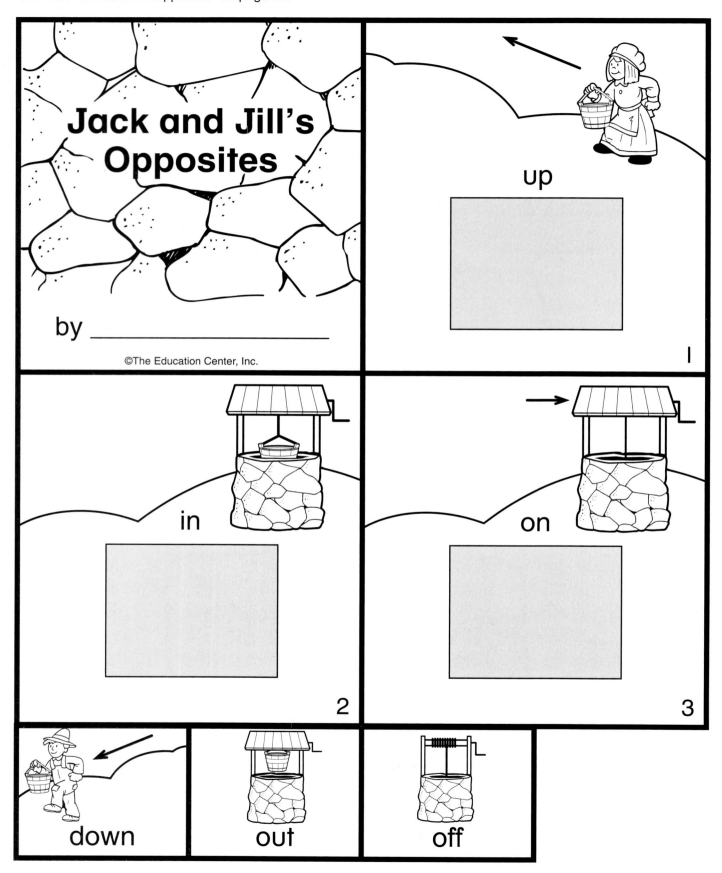

Jack and Jill's Opposites

by _____

©The Education Center, Inc.

up

I

in

2

on

3

down

out

Jill tumbling

Jack tumbling

Booklet Pages and Opposites Cards

Use with "A 'Well-th' of Opposites" on page 83.

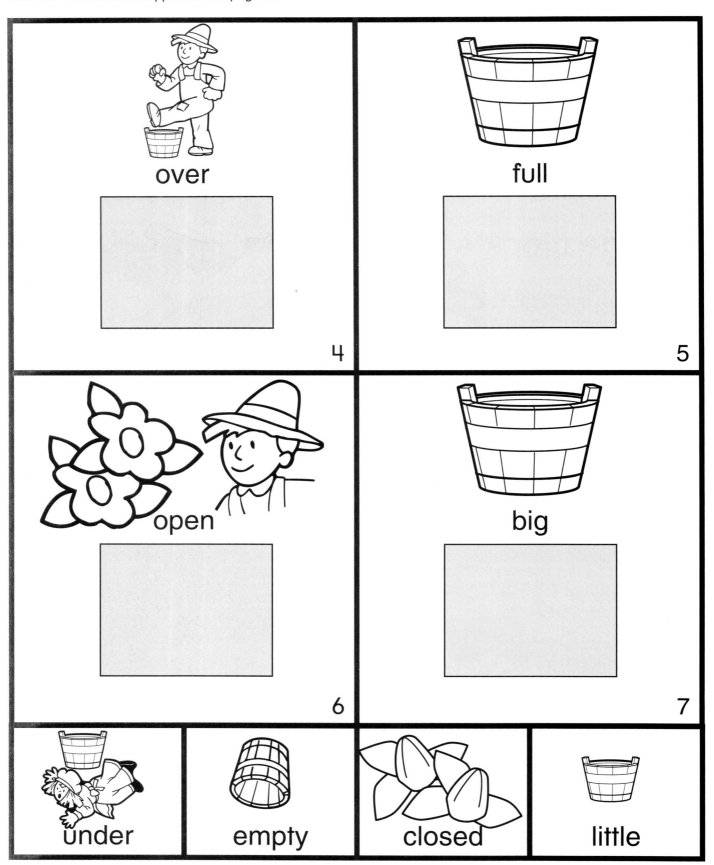

over

full

4

5

open

big

6

7

under

empty

closed

little

Hickory, Dickory, Dock

Hickory, dickory, dock,

The mouse ran up the clock.

The clock struck one;

The mouse ran down,

Hickory, dickory, dock.

Hickory, Dickory, Dock

Hickory, dickory, dock,

The mouse ran up the clock.

The clock struck one;

The mouse ran down,

Hickory, dickory, dock.

Hickory, Dickory, Dock

When the clock strikes one, it's time for nursery rhyme fun! Engage your students with these lively activities featuring mice, clocks, and more!

Let's Learn About Clocks!
Building on prior knowledge

This timely discussion will have your youngsters chiming in with their knowledge of clocks and such. In advance, gather several different types of timepieces: digital clocks, watches, windup clocks, stopwatches, cuckoo clocks, and so forth. Display these timekeepers for your group during circle time and invite each child to explore them. Discuss similarities and differences in shape, sound, and use; then group them accordingly. Also prompt each child to decide where each type of clock could be found. Next, show students a picture of a grandfather clock and describe its large size and loud chime. Then use the poster on page 91 and the accompanying patterns to introduce the nursery rhyme. Ticktock!

dock, clock
mouse, house
hickory, dickory
one, fun
clue, blue
sun, run
bear, wear

Rhyme Chimes
Recognizing rhyming words

Grandfather clocks chime the hour with big, beautiful sounds—so blend chimes and rhymes for an experience that will keep everyone's attention! Encourage each child to pretend to be a grandfather clock waiting to chime. Give each child a rhythm instrument and ask her to hold it quietly until she hears a rhyming pair of words. Then, in the ticktock rhythm of a clock, slowly say pairs of words. Include some pairs that rhyme and some that don't (see the list for suggestions). When a child hears a rhyming pair, she chimes her instrument. For more advanced learners, have each child take a turn supplying a rhyme for your spoken word while the rest of the group chimes agreement.

Name That Sound!
Recognizing beginning sounds

These fuzzy little mice will repeatedly run up and down clocks to help your little ones listen for beginning sounds! In advance, make enough copies of the clock pattern on page 98 for a small group. Give each child in a small group a clock pattern and a cotton ball to represent a mouse. Have him place the cotton ball at the bottom of his clock and listen as you say various words. When he hears a word that begins with an /r/ sound (see the list of suggested words below), he makes his mouse "run" up the clock. The next time he hears an /r/ word, he makes his mouse "run" back down the clock. Run, run, little mousie!

run rabbit rock rag roll rub roast rack rib roam

Words, Words Everywhere
Segmenting sentences into words

What's in a word? Letters, of course! This quick and easy activity will provide your youngsters with plenty of practice segmenting sentences into words. In advance, make a class supply of page 92. Using the poster, show students the word *hickory* and the spaces

around it; then explain that words are groups of letters with spaces around them. Further explain that you need each student's help to find all the words in this nursery rhyme. Ask each child to use a yellow crayon to circle each word on her copy of page 92. When students finish, invite each child to take a turn using a wipe-off pen to circle a word on the laminated poster. Congratulate your word detectives on a job well done!

Mouse Run!
Associating letters with sounds

Help the mouse get to the clock in this fun partner game! In advance, photocopy the gameboard halves on pages 100 and 102. Color the halves as desired, cut them out, and assemble the board. Glue it to a file folder or sheet of tagboard. Laminate the gameboard; then store it in a center with two different-colored pom-poms and a paper bag containing three number cards labeled "1," "2," and "3." To play, a child selects a pom-pom mouse and places it on start. She reaches into the bag, selects one number card, and reads it. She moves her mouse that number of spaces and reads the word on which she lands. If her word begins with the letter *m,* she takes another turn. If her word does not begin with *m,* her turn ends. The second player takes a turn in this same manner. The first player to reach the clock is the winner. For more advanced learners, set a kitchen timer for a desired amount of time; then challenge players to reach the clock before it chimes. Come on, *m!*

Chiming the Hour
Strengthening number awareness

Here's a timely way to practice listening and number skills—nursery rhyme style! To prepare, program each of five sticky notes with a different numeral from 1 to 5. Give each child in a small group a rhythm instrument and direct her attention to the poster. Read the rhyme aloud, inviting students to chime the hour when appropriate. Next, cover the word *one* with a preprogrammed sticky note. Read the rhyme again, substituting the new number and inviting students to play a matching number of chimes. Hey! The clock struck four!

Marvelous Mice
Following oral directions, retelling a story

Hurry, scurry—everyone will want to make these adorable mouse puppets! Invite each child to paint the backs of two seven-inch paper plates with gray washable tempera paint. When the paint is dry, staple the plates together, leaving an opening for the child's hand as shown. Have each child glue on construction paper ears, a yarn tail, pom-pom eyes, and a pom-pom nose. Then invite each child to draw whiskers with a crayon or maker. Pair students and have one child in each pair pretend to be the clock. Have the other child use her mouse puppet to retell and act out the rhyme. Then invite students to switch roles and play again. These mice are welcome in any classroom!

Ticktock Cookie Clocks
Following oral directions

Any time is the right time to make these tasty timepieces! To make one, give a child a slice of refrigerated sugar cookie dough and a personalized five-inch square of aluminum foil. Lightly spray the foil with cooking spray; then have the child place his dough slice on the foil. Give him 12 mini chocolate chips and have him arrange them around the edge of the dough to resemble clock numbers. Then have him place two one-inch pieces of red string licorice on his cookie to resemble clock hands at one o'clock. Bake as directed, let the cookies cool, and then serve them with cups of cold milk. It's time to snack!

Jaaron

Glue here.

Patterns

Use with "Hickory, Dickory, Dock" on pages 91–96.

clock

mouse

©The Education Center, Inc. • *Once Upon a Nursery Rhyme* • TEC1113

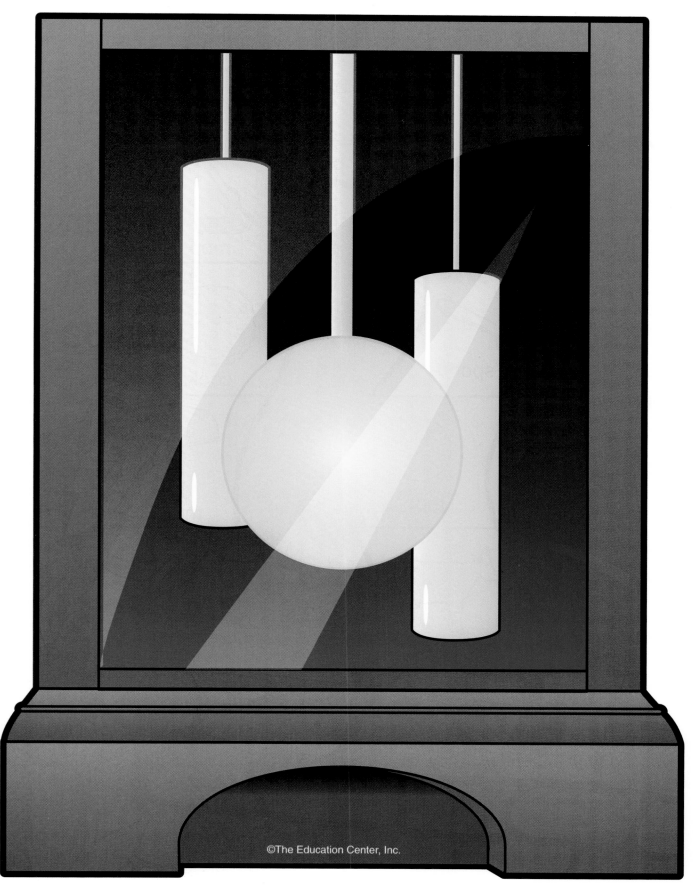

Gameboard Half

Use with "Mouse Run!" on page 95 and the gameboard half on page 102.

Help the mouse get to the clock!

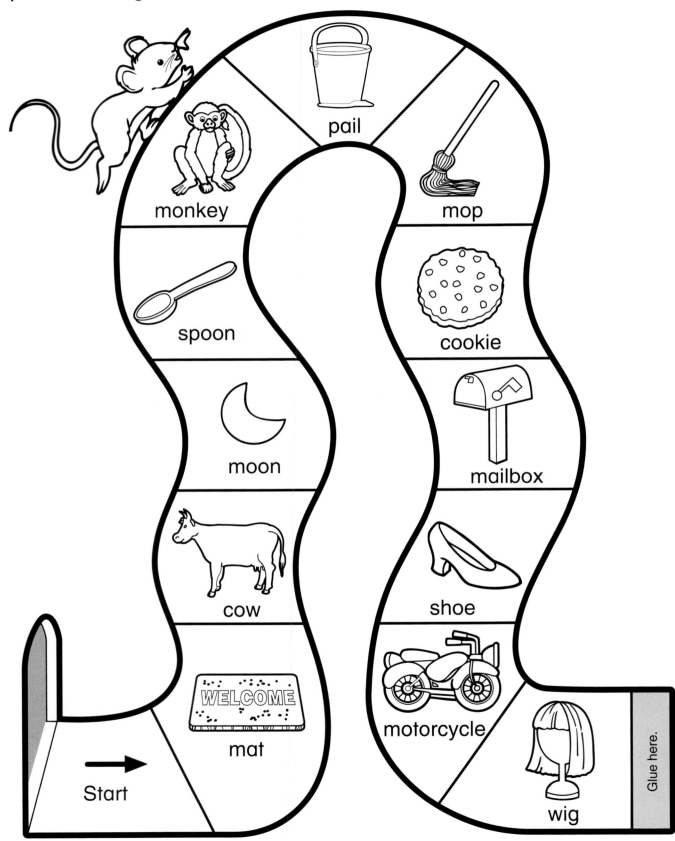

monkey

pail

mop

spoon

cookie

moon

mailbox

cow

shoe

WELCOME

mat

Start

motorcycle

wig

Glue here.

Gameboard Half

Use with "Mouse Run!" on page 95 and the gameboard half on page 100.

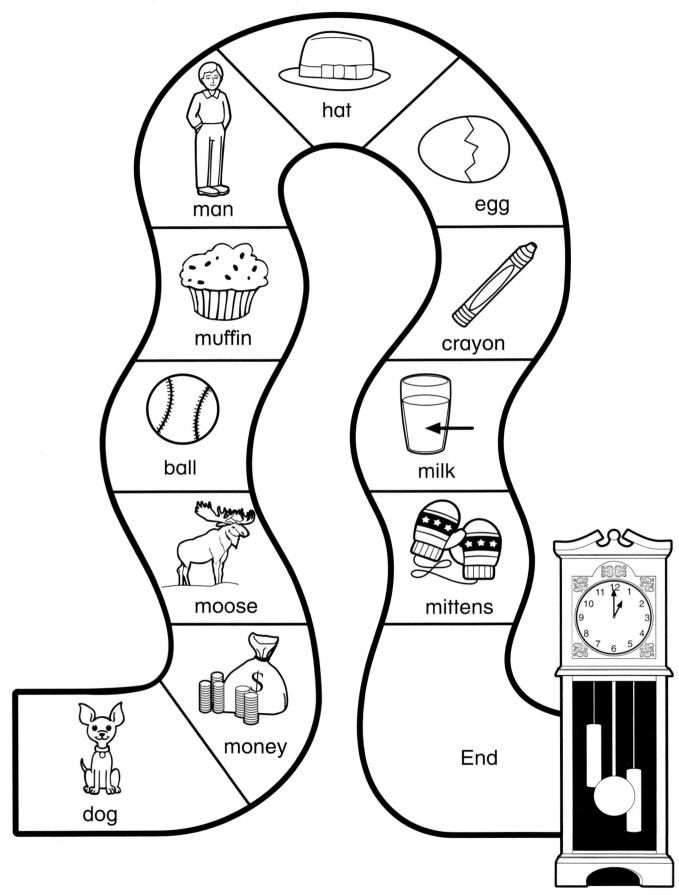

man

hat

egg

muffin

crayon

ball

milk

moose

mittens

money

End

dog

©The Education Center, Inc. • *Once Upon a Nursery Rhyme* • TEC1113

Little Bo-Peep

Little Bo-Peep has lost her sheep

And can't tell where to find them.

Leave them alone,

And they'll come home,

Wagging their tails behind them.

Little Bo-Peep

Little Bo-Peep has lost her sheep

And can't tell where to find them.

Leave them alone,

And they'll come home,

Wagging their tails behind them.

Little Bo-Peep

Your little lambs won't be lost after they've completed some of these engaging activities! So gather your flock for a lot of learning with Little Bo-Peep.

Woolly Wisdom
Building on prior knowledge

Don't let anyone pull the wool over your little lambs' eyes! Empower youngsters' sense of self as they review ways to stay safe with this activity. Begin by discussing with students the meaning of the word *lost.* Ask youngsters to share ideas about what to do if separated from a parent in a store or at a park. Guide students to understand that they need to memorize personal information (full name, address, telephone number) to use in an emergency. Help each child record her personal information on a copy of the lamb on page 112. Have each child repeat her personal information and attach a sticker to each known item. Then use the poster on page 103 and the accompanying patterns to share Little Bo-Peep with your little flock. Afterward, encourage each child to take her little lamb home to review with her family.

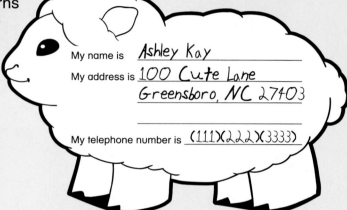

My name is *Ashley Kay*
My address is *100 Cute Lane*
Greensboro, NC 27403

My telephone number is *(111)(222)(3333)*

Little Lamb Sounds
Identifying beginning sound /l/

Your little lambs will "baa" with joy over this listening activity. Begin by sharing the rhyme with youngsters. Then introduce the /l/ sound and ask youngsters to repeat the sound. Have students listen as you read the rhyme again and ask them to say "baa" each time they hear a word that begins with /l/. Invite each child to share a different word with a beginning /l/ sound and record her answer on a chart. Then say a group of words to youngsters (using some from the chart) and ask them to "baa" each time they hear a word beginning with /l/. What a "baa-tiful" sound!

baa

Gathering Sheep

Identifying onsets and rimes, blending sounds to make words

Invite your little shepherds to gather some very special sheep! In advance, mask the text on a copy of the pattern on page 112 and then make a class supply of construction paper sheep. Cut out each pattern and then cut each one in half. Program the front half of each sheep with an onset and the other half with a rime as shown. If desired, laminate each set for durability. Then hide the front half of each sheep in your classroom.

To begin the activity, ask each child to find the front half of a little lost sheep and then return to the group. Ask one child at a time to say the beginning sound and name the letter on his sheep. Next, give him the corresponding rime half of the sheep. Then help him name the rime and blend the two sounds to create a word. If desired, place the sheep sets in a center for further practice. Little Bo-Peep would admire your youngsters' herding *and* reading abilities!

Grazing Left to Right

Tracking print from left to right

Introduce youngsters to the concept of reading from left to right with these word-munching sheep puppets! To prepare, make a class supply of the rhyme poster on page 104. Also duplicate the sheep pattern (shown) on page 110 on tagboard for each child. Have each child cut out her sheep pattern. Then help each child make a finger puppet by attaching the sheep to a finger-size roll of paper as shown. Tell youngsters that these are special reading sheep, which only eat from left to right. With finger puppets in place, invite each child to point to each word on her copy as you read the rhyme aloud. Check to make sure youngsters are tracking left to right and using return sweep to get to the beginning of each new rhyme line. Then invite pairs of students to use their puppets to take turns reading and tracking the rhyme. Just watch these hungry sheep lead your little ones to learning fun!

Name ___Alex___   *Story Starter*

Little Bo-Peep has lost her sheep,
and ___Alex___ knows where to find them!
A sheep is hiding ___undr the trampolin!___.

Creative Wandering
Creative thinking, writing to complete a sentence

Inspire creative thinking as your youngsters write about Little Bo-Peep's wandering sheep. In advance, make a copy of page 114 for each child. Then gather a small group of students to discuss the rhyme. Encourage each child to pretend he is helping Little Bo-Peep find her sheep. Ask him to think of a place where the sheep might be hiding. Then have him write or dictate to complete the sentences on a copy of page 114. Have each child illustrate his sentences in the space provided. Later, gather all the pages and staple them together with a cover titled "Our Wandering Sheep." Share the book with youngsters and then place it in your reading center for your little flock to enjoy.

A Colorful Flock
Sorting, counting, creating a class graph

This colorful graphing activity will surely lead your flock to fun! Use the sheep pattern (shown) on page 110 to make a class supply of sheep in four colors. Cut out the sheep. Also create a class graph, similar to the one shown, substituting color words to match your colored sheep. Then hide the colored sheep around your classroom.

To begin the activity, invite each child to find one sheep and return to the circle area. Then help youngsters sort themselves into four separate groups according to their sheep's colors. Have each group count its sheep. Have one group at a time use tape to attach its sheep to the corresponding section of the graph. When each group is finished, count the number of sheep in each color section together. Ask one student from each group to write the correct number of sheep at the bottom of the corresponding section as shown. Then review the graph with youngsters, discussing which color group had the most and which had the least.

A Colorful Flock

red	yellow	green	blue
10	4	3	7

Little Sheep, Follow Me!
Counting, strengthening observation and memory skills

Count on this memory game to get your little lambs wagging their tails with excitement! To prepare, arrange six chairs in a line in an open area of your classroom. Tell youngsters they will pretend to be characters from the rhyme as they play. First, choose one child to play Little Bo-Peep and ask her to choose six little sheep to sit in the chairs. Ask Little Bo-Peep to turn away from her flock. Then quietly tap several children to hide in a predetermined location. Then say "Little [leader's name]-Peep, count your sheep!" Allow time for the leader to count the empty chairs and then ask her to respond with "I've lost [number missing] sheep!" Challenge the leader to identify each missing child. Then repeat the game several times with a different leader each time.

Home for a Herd
Understanding the basic needs of animals, dramatic play

Herd your youngsters together for a discussion about taking care of Little Bo-Peep's fuzzy friends. To prepare, stock your dramatic-play center with some sheepherding props (hats, bandanas, work gloves, etc.). Stock your block center with small plastic farm toys (corrals, sheep, other farm animals), green crinkle paper (to represent food), and plastic tubs (to represent water).

Discuss the basic needs of animals with youngsters. Guide them to understand that sheep need food, water, and shelter to live. Invite a few youngsters at a time to dress up as shepherds and then create a corral for their sheep. Remind your little shepherds to feed and water their flock. Bet these sheep are glad to be home!

©The Education Center, Inc.

Patterns

Use with "Little Bo-Peep" on pages 103–108.

Little Bo-Peep

sheep

©The Education Center, Inc.

©The Education Center, Inc.

Sheep Pattern
Use with "Woolly Wisdom" on page 105 and "Gathering Sheep" on page 106.

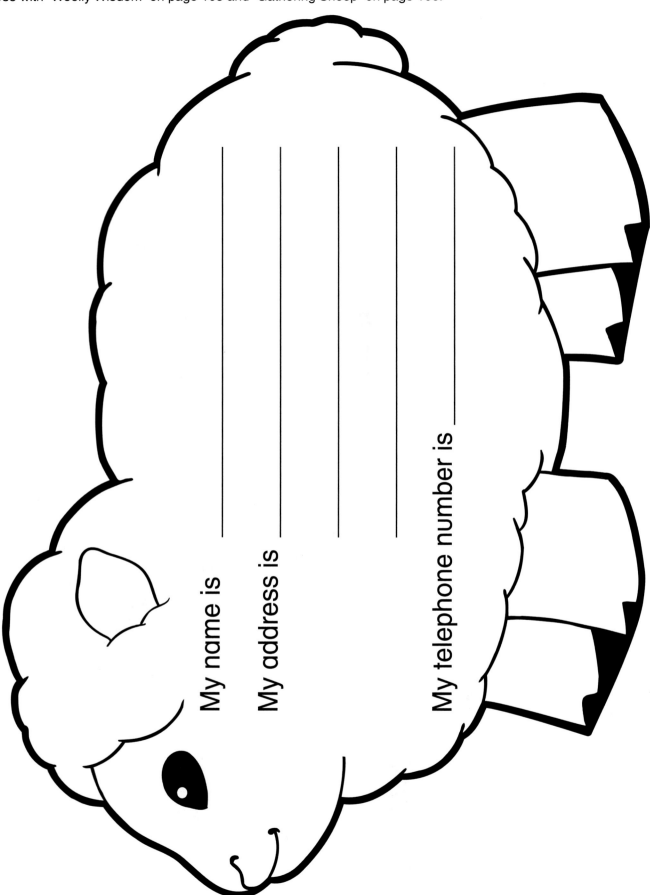

My name is _____

My address is _____

My telephone number is _____

©The Education Center, Inc.

©The Education Center, Inc.

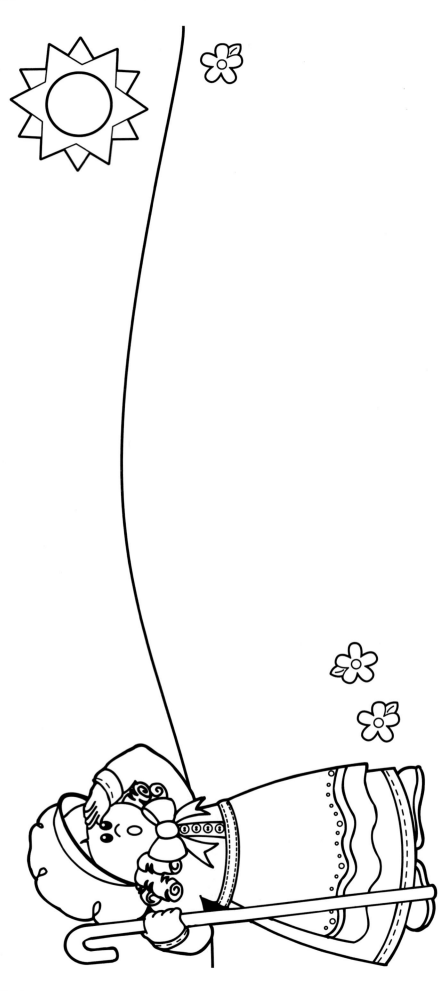

Little Bo-Peep has lost her sheep,

and _____ knows where to find them!

A sheep is hiding _____ .

Note to the teacher: Use with "Creative Wandering" on page 107.

Three Little Kittens

Three little kittens
They lost their mittens,
And they began to cry,
"Oh, Mother Dear,
We sadly fear
Our mittens we have lost!"

"What? Lost your mittens?
You naughty kittens!
Then you shall have no pie."
"Meow, meow, meow!"

The three little kittens
Found their mittens,
And they began to cry,
"Oh, Mother Dear,
See here, see here!
Our mittens we have found."

"What? Found your mittens?
You good little kittens!
Then you shall have some pie."
"Purr, purr, purr."

Three Little Kittens

Three little kittens
They lost their mittens,
And they began to cry,
"Oh, Mother Dear,
We sadly fear
Our mittens we have lost!"

"What? Lost your mittens?
You naughty kittens!
Then you shall have no pie."
"Meow, meow, meow!"

The three little kittens
Found their mittens,
And they began to cry,
"Oh, Mother Dear,
See here, see here!
Our mittens we have found."

"What? Found your mittens?
You good little kittens!
Then you shall have some pie."
"Purr, purr, purr."

Three Little Kittens

What happens when you have three forgetful kittens, a disappointed mother cat, and the promise of missed dessert? Why, those kittens go find their mittens, and everything ends happily ever after!

Lost and Found

Building on prior knowledge

Have you ever lost something? Invite students to ponder this question and then lead them in a discussion of what items are commonly lost. Ask volunteers to reveal how they feel when they lose things they like. Then have each student think about a treasured item she has recently lost. Give each child a copy of the "Lost!" poster on page 124 and invite her to write (or dictate) to complete the sentences. Next, encourage her to illustrate her missing item in the space provided. Display the completed sheets on a bulletin board titled "Lost and Found." Then tell youngsters that you know of three little kittens who lost their mittens. Use the poster on page 115 and the accompanying patterns to share the nursery rhyme. Meow, meow, meow!

Lost!

I have lost   my bear

If found, please tell   Gabbie

Kitten Capers

Retelling a story

Now showing at a puppet theater near you—Kitten Capers! Starring story retelling skills and produced with lots of fun, these miniplays will captivate your youngsters! To begin, enlarge and duplicate page 122 onto construction paper to make a class supply. Have each child make puppets by coloring the patterns, cutting them out, and taping each to a different craft stick. Divide children into groups of three. Encourage students in each group to use their puppets to sequence and retell the story of the three kittens. Then invite each group, in turn, to take its place inside a puppet theater and retell the story to the class. Shhh—the curtain is going up!

Lost Sounds
Deleting initial phonemes
What in the world happens when the first sound in a word is lost? Sometimes a different word is found! Give your older students a chance to delete beginning phonemes in this lost-and-found sound activity. Say a word (see the list for suggestions); then have students repeat it. Ask a volunteer to identify the beginning sound. Say the word again, delete the first phoneme, and then say the resulting word. Repeat the activity in this same manner with a different word. For more challenge, invite students to predict the resulting word before you say it aloud. Lose the first sound, and another word is found!

mother
box
dear
cat
ball
hair
tape
fan
gate
for

Dear. Take off d and you have ear!

Who Said That?
Recognizing quotation marks
When you're reading, how can you tell when a character is speaking? Quotation marks give it away every time! Develop your youngsters' awareness of these useful little marks with some fun speech bubbles. In advance, put the prepared color character patterns and a white felt speech bubble on a flannelboard. Using the color poster, read the rhyme aloud and point out the quotation marks as they arise. Afterward, ask students what they think the marks do. Lead students to conclude that the marks tell the reader when a character is talking. Read the rhyme again, pausing at each quotation mark to place the speech bubble above the appropriate character. For more challenge, read the narrative parts aloud; when you reach dialogue, invite a student volunteer to hold the speech bubble above the appropriate character and speak the words. Those little marks are a giveaway every time!

The Continuing Saga of the Three Kittens
Demonstrating story comprehension

Picture a class book that shows how well your little ones understand the story of the three kittens. In advance, copy each line of
the nursery rhyme onto a different sheet
of 12" x 18" construction paper. Read the
rhyme aloud; then give each child one of
the programmed sheets and read the text
to her. Direct her to carefully think about the
text and then illustrate it. Invite each child
to share her finished page, and then stack
the pages in order and bind them between
two covers to create a class book. Read the
book aloud before placing it in your class
library for further student enjoyment. Purr,
purr, purr.

"Our mittens we have found."

For more mitten matching practice, invite each
child to complete a copy of page 126.

Clothesline Classification
Sorting and classifying

Laundry is a welcome treat when it
involves sorting and matching mittens!
Cut pairs of mittens from wallpaper
samples. Hang a yarn clothesline
within easy student reach and store
the mittens and a supply of clothespins in a plastic basket nearby. Invite
visitors to this center to dump out the
mittens, match them, and then use
clothespins to hang the pairs on the
clothesline. After you've checked their
work, invite students to take the mittens
off the line and store them in the laundry
basket. What tidy kittens!

Seasonal Style
Comparing seasonal clothing

Mittens are often considered winter wear, but what might the three little kittens wear in spring? Raincoats? Sweaters? Adapt the familiar nursery rhyme for some seasonal fun! To begin, program a chart with the four seasons, and ask students during which season the kittens would need mittens. Lead youngsters to conclude that winter is the best time for mittens. Write the word "mittens" in the winter quadrant. Then ask students to think of other clothing items and the season when each is best worn. Record student suggestions on the chart. After several responses, choose one and substitute it for *mittens* in the rhyme. Continue repeating the rhyme, substituting other suggested clothing, until everyone is wearing a smile. Then, whenever you have a spare minute, revisit this activity for clothing comparisons that are perfect in any season!

Winter	Spring
mittens hats coats	raincoats boots
Summer	**Fall**
flip-flops shorts bathing suits	sweaters

Savory Survey
Understanding a picture graph

Oh, my! What delicious pie! Find out what type of pie your little ones prefer with this tasty graph. In advance, purchase three kinds of canned pie filling. Also purchase enough baked mini fillo dough shells (available in grocery stores) for each child to have three. On a sheet of bulletin board paper, program a three-column graph with the kinds of fillings (see example). Make a class supply of the pie patterns on page 128 and cut them apart. Just before beginning the activity, fill the shells so that each child has one of each flavor. Serve each child his pies. Encourage him to taste each pie and choose his favorite. Next, help him write his name and the name of his preferred flavor on a pie pattern, then lightly color the pie to match. Show students the graph and invite each child, in turn, to add his pie pattern to the appropriate column. Discuss the results as a class. It's as easy as pie!

We Like Pie!

| cherry | blueberry | apple |

©The Education Center, Inc.

©The Education Center, Inc.

©The Education Center, Inc.

Patterns

Use with "Three Little Kittens" on pages 115–120.

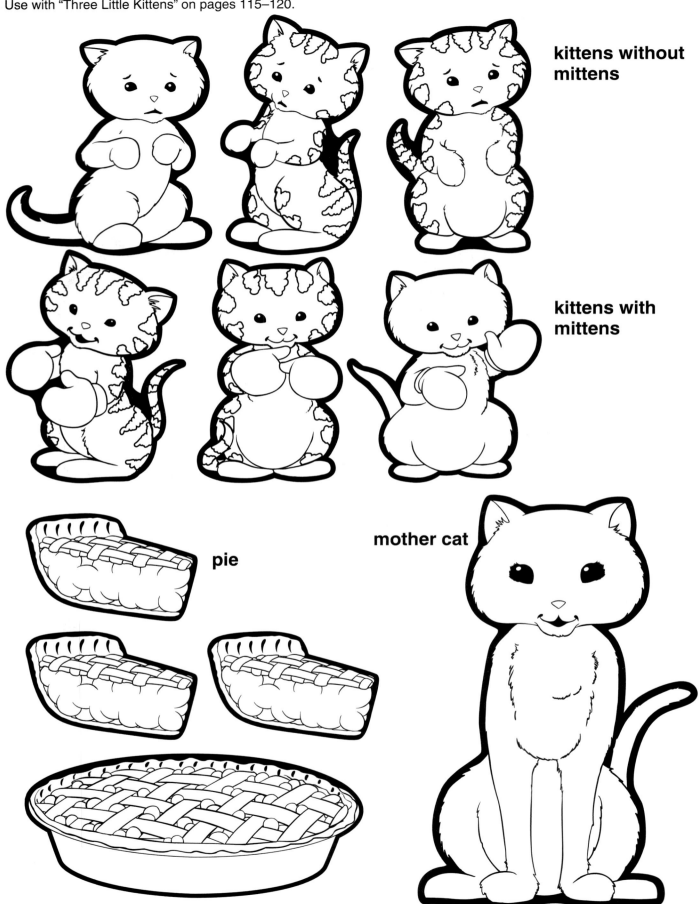

kittens without mittens

kittens with mittens

pie

mother cat

©The Education Center, Inc.

©The Education Center, Inc.

©The Education Center, Inc.

Lost!

I have lost _____.

If found, please tell _____.

Note to the teacher: Use with "Lost and Found" on page 117.

©The Education Center, Inc.

Name

Laundry Day

✂ Cut.

Match.

Glue.

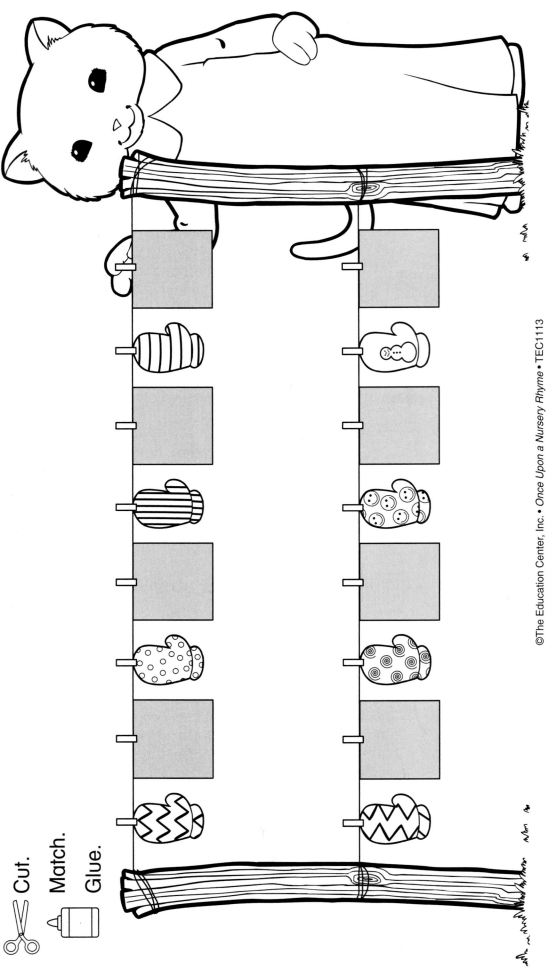

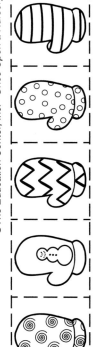

Pie Patterns

Use with "Three Little Kittens" on page 115 and "Who Said That?" on page 118.

©The Education Center, Inc.

©The Education Center, Inc.

©The Education Center, Inc.

©The Education Center, Inc.

©The Education Center, Inc. • *Once Upon a Nursery Rhyme* • TEC1113   127

Recording Sheets
Use with "Savory Survey" on page 120.

I like _____ pie!

_____
Name

I like _____ pie!

_____
Name